Furniture:
a Concise History

Edward Lucie-Smith

OXFORD UNIVERSITY PRESS

NEW YORK AND TORONTO

1979

For John Makepeace

Frontispiece: Hoffmann, two armchairs. Black and
white wash, 1903

Library of Congress Cataloging in Publication Data
Lucie-Smith, Edward.
  Furniture.

  (World of art series)
  Bibliography: p.
  Includes index.
  1. Furniture–History. I. Title.
NK2270.L82 1979   749.2   79–4393
ISBN 0–19–520145–0
ISBN 0–19–520146–9 pbk.

Printed and bound in Great Britain by
Jarrold and Sons Ltd, Norwich

Contents

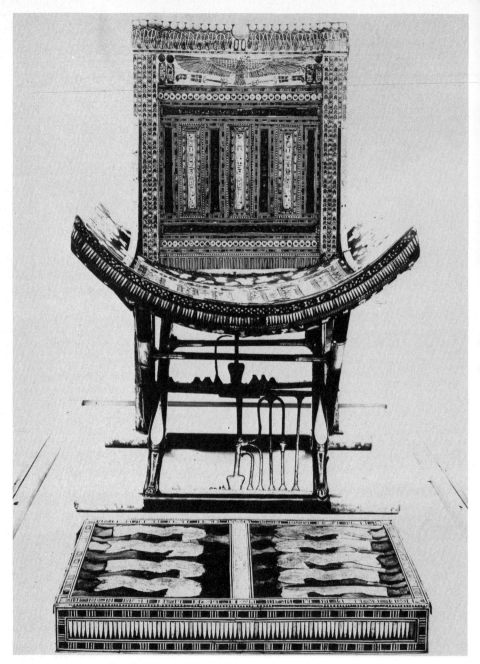

1 Inlaid throne from the tomb of the Pharaoh Tutankhamun, Thebes, *c.* 1350 BC

CHAPTER ONE

Meanings of furniture

Furniture occupies a curiously ambiguous place among human artefacts. Strictly speaking, it is not necessary to human existence; and some cultures, more especially nomadic ones, seem to get on well enough without it. Because of its bulk, most furniture implies a reasonably settled existence. Indeed, at one end of the scale, it is almost inseparable from architecture. Built-in furniture, often thought of in this century as typically 'modern', is in fact the earliest we know – a neolithic house at Skara Brae in the Orkneys incorporates built-in 2 seats and sleeping-places.

But the possession of articles of furniture does, nevertheless, imply a level of culture some way above the subsistence level, just as it implies an abandonment of animal habits and postures. In this respect, seat-furniture is perhaps the most significant, since the use of a stool or chair to sit on implies that the user has been educated by his or her cultural surroundings. It does not, on the other hand, in itself imply

2 Prehistoric stone house at Skara Brae, Orkney, with built-in benches and sleeping-spaces

cultural superiority. The stool and the chair have a long and continuous history in Western Europe and in the Near East, but are distinctly exotic in India, and are by no means universally employed in China and Japan. The implications of these differences are so far-reaching that this book will, for the sake of clarity and simplicity, confine itself to the two regions first mentioned – that is, broadly speaking, to the tradition in which most of its readers are likely to have grown up (for my purposes, what has happened in the Americas since the period of European settlement can be treated as part of the same general development).

If one considers the broader implications of the subject, it becomes apparent that furniture can be thought of, no matter what its period, under four different headings.

The first is obvious: one thinks of it in terms of function, and these practical functions are in fact comparatively few. One sits on a piece of furniture (stools, benches and chairs); or else one puts things on it (tables and stands); sleeps or reclines on it (beds and couches); or uses it for storage (chests and wardrobes). As will be seen from quite a number of illustrations in this book, these functions are sometimes combined, but more often there will occur a fine differentiation within a given category, so that a piece of furniture acquires its definitive form through being designed to meet a single, utterly specific and highly specialized need.

The eighteenth century is prolific in furniture of this type. An example which comes to mind is the kind of chair called a *voyeuse*, made for the use of spectators at a card-game. Indeed, there is in this case a further refinement – there are two types of *voyeuse*, one for men and one for women. The man's, often miscalled in English a cock-fighting chair, is designed so that he sits astride, facing what would normally be the back, which is waisted so as to accommodate his legs, meanwhile resting his arms on a padded rail. The woman, because of her skirts, cannot be expected to seat herself in this way, and therefore kneels upon a seat which is lowered for the purpose, though she too is provided with a padded rail on which to rest her forearms. But the invention of the *voyeuse* was inspired by the misuse of an ordinary upright chair.

The second heading is one of which furniture historians are now increasingly conscious: furniture plays a very important part as an indicator of social status. The more hierarchical the society, the

3

3 A *bergère voyeuse* by Jean Baptiste
Tilliard, 1752

greater the emphasis on this particular role, so that questions of
convenience or comfort are often entirely usurped by it. Indeed,
furniture is only marginally less important than clothes and personal
adornments as a means of conveying this sort of information.

A third method of approach is to consider furniture from the
technological aspect. But, while this provides quite a good measure of
technological progress, especially in the nineteenth and twentieth
centuries, certain things have to be taken into account. One is that
until comparatively recently making furniture was a craft rather than
an industry, and the technology concerned was a matter of the degree
of skill with which one particular material was handled, e.g. wood.
There was by no means a steady progression in this respect. The
furniture found in Tutankhamun's tomb, for instance, is, from the
point of view of craftsmanship, more refined than anything produced
in Europe from the beginning of the middle ages until the mid
eighteenth century.

The actual materials used for furniture, the types of wood and so
forth, do undoubtedly tell us certain things quite clearly. Mahogany,

for instance, became the favourite material among English furniture-makers just as the British colonial empire began to expand. In order to buy British manufactures, the colonies needed to send raw materials in return. Mahogany, hard, worm-proof and finer in grain than most native woods, was one of the things they sent.

It is true to say, however, that the real technological revolution has overtaken furniture-making only comparatively recently, and is still going on. Furniture-making techniques, and even the materials considered suitable for the purpose, have changed more drastically in the past sixty years than they did in the six preceding centuries. This is one reason for devoting so much space to twentieth-century furniture in this book.

The fourth category that I want to examine is the way in which furniture is used to make a purely personal and subjective statement about the individual who chooses to live with it. Furniture is the servant of fantasy just as much as it is a response to practical everyday needs. The whole notion of the domestic interior as scenery for a play

4 Nineteenth-century furniture arrangement. A room at Canford Manor, Dorset, decorated in about 1847

5 Eighteenth-century furniture arrangement. The Long Gallery at Osterley, Middlesex

6 Eighteenth-century furniture arrangement. Parlour of the Peyton Randolph House, Colonial Williamsburg, Virginia

which we make up as we go along, and therefore of pieces of furniture as components in a constantly shifting and capriciously altered three-dimensional collage, is propagated today in every interior decorating magazine. Its roots lie deep in the eighteenth century, with individualists like Horace Walpole and William Beckford, and it established itself firmly in the nineteenth, when multiplicity of stylistic choice led eventually to a breakdown of previously fixed categories, a kind of overflowing from one compartment to another which can be seen in many contemporary representations of Victorian interiors. It was at this time that isolated examples of old furniture acquired the kind of talismanic force which many people attach to them today, and became the foci for ideas and emotions which were not necessarily connected with their appearance.

The study of furniture, which arose from the antiquarian interests of the nineteenth century, has ever since been bedevilled by an obsession with 'antiques'. Though this book is concerned with the history of furniture, it has little to do with the questions of identification and genuineness with which studies of the subject usually concern themselves. It tries, instead, to show how furniture is related to the general development of society, and also to the psychology of the individual.

In order to understand the furniture of the past it is essential to consider, not merely the kind of statement which each piece in isolation makes about those who bought and commissioned it, but the whole question of its arrangement. In fact, as can be seen from old photographs, it was perfectly possible to transform a classic eighteenth-century interior, with nearly all its contents intact, merely by rearranging what was in the room to suit new needs and new ideas about social intercourse. The question of furniture arrangement is one to which historians of the subject have also been devoting increasing attention, and the result has been not only the publication of some fascinating books, but practical attempts at re-creation such as Ham House and Osterley in England, Malmaison in France, and the uncannily convincing interiors at Colonial Williamsburg in the United States.

These studies and their offshoots have up to now been valued chiefly for the information they provide about the way people lived from day to day, how they ordered their lives, and the kind of expectations they had of one another. How did people amuse

4

5, 107
6

12

themselves after dinner? And where and when did they eat? A study of furniture, or an attempt to reconstitute an actual interior, can provide us with many details. Match the furniture itself with accounts, diaries, letters and descriptions of all kinds, and an almost complete picture emerges.

Yet it has to be recognized that these studies would not be so necessary if there had not been a break in the psychological continuity of European society. It is a matter of controversy when this break took place. Some people assign it to the Industrial Revolution. In fact, it seems to have happened after the beginning of that revolution in the mid eighteenth century, but before its effects were fully felt. The year 1800 is as good a choice as any. Nineteenth-century revivalism is an attempt to discover and rescue an elusive past. Rebellions against that revivalism – first the Arts and Crafts Movement, then Art Nouveau, then the committed modernism which came from De Stijl and the Bauhaus on one hand, and Le Corbusier and L'Esprit Nouveau on the other – are significant not only in their own right but because of the thing they react against.

The temptation is to classify everything before the gap as 'old' and everything after it as more or less 'modern'. Antique-dealers, for instance, sometimes insist that nothing is antique which was made after 1830, though the barrier has been broken down in recent years by the enthusiasm of collectors for Art Nouveau and Art Deco. In fact, furniture has been becoming history faster than historians can write it. The rebellious movements I have just named did much to create the interiors we live in today. Yet, though we speak of them as 'modern', the most recent are no longer contemporary. The Bauhaus and Le Corbusier are now just as much a part of the history of furniture as the stylistic innovations of a Chippendale or a Hepplewhite.

One of the fascinations of furniture history is that its perspectives are constantly shifting. History often serves as a basis for prophecy. Indeed, many people would say it is the only possible basis. A few years ago, anyone writing a book on this theme would probably have been convinced that things were coming full circle – that the earliest furniture was completely built in; and that the most recent would be completely built in too; that furniture was a limb cut off from architecture, and was now about to be joined again to the body from which it had been severed. Many things, logic not least, support this

7 English Gothic cupboard of about
1500, with architectural decoration

point of view. Furniture, from the middle ages onwards, has
constantly been influenced by architecture. Ornament on furniture is,
more often than not, borrowed from this source. Architects, certainly
from the eighteenth century onwards, have exercised an enormous
influence over the way in which furniture has developed, insisting
that there ought to be a unity between interior architecture and the
5   objects placed within a given space. The names of Robert Adam and
141   Charles Rennie Mackintosh are only two of the many that come to
mind in this connection.

Today I am not convinced that built-in furniture is the inevitable
and only solution to the problems of modern living. I believe, rather,
that furniture will keep its own identity; and that, far from being
challenged by architecture, it is now in a position to offer a challenge
to sculpture. One of the things the Modern Movement has done is to
teach us to look at forms more attentively, in isolation from their
function, and also from what they may or may not represent. This
means that we look at an artefact such as a chair with entirely new

14

eyes. If it is old, we are conscious not only of the talismanic properties I have already mentioned, but of its qualities as pure form. If it is new, we automatically compare it to the contemporary sculpture it so closely resembles. Furniture therefore tends to separate itself from its background, rather than blend in with it. Because we focus more exactly when we look at it, we are increasingly aware of details of workmanship, as well as of the strength or weakness of the form itself. The revival of craftsmanship which I discuss in my final chapter is due not only to a revulsion against the alternate blandness or shoddiness of the machine-made, but to this change in our point of view. One of my over-all objectives in writing this book is to show precisely by what stages the change has come about.

9

8

8 Calder, stabile. *Le Petit Nez*, black metal, 1959

9 Armchair in moulded plastic reinforced with fibreglass, by Eames, 1951

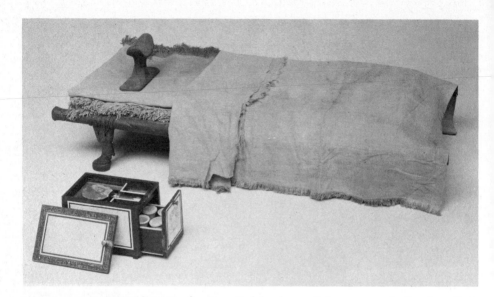

10 Ancient Egyptian furniture. Bed, headrest and silver-mounted toilet-chest. Early Dynastic

11 Ancient Egyptian furniture. Gold-mounted carrying-chair of Queen Hetepheres. 4th Dynasty

CHAPTER TWO

Ancient Egypt, Western Asia, Greece and Rome

The earliest specimens of furniture known to us are among the most elaborate. This is due, very largely, to the circumstances in which they have been preserved – in the tombs of the highest dignitaries of Ancient Egypt. Egyptian burial customs, which insisted that all material luxuries must be provided for the departed in his or her future life, together with an exceedingly dry climate, have seen to it that many items have survived more or less intact. The basic range includes tables, stools, chairs, beds, and also storage chests of various *10* shapes and sizes.

Little complete furniture of any kind survives from the Early Dynastic period of *c.* 3100–*c.* 2700 BC, but there are enough fragments to indicate that the Egyptian upper class already enjoyed a high standard of luxury. Among these fragments are a series of carved ivory bull's legs, which were evidently used as supports for stools, couches and small chests. It is startling to find that the convention of the animal-leg support, which we now associate with much later epochs, and most of all with the great English and French cabinet-makers of the eighteenth century, began thus early.

The furniture of Queen Hetepheres, wife of Sneferu, the first pharaoh of the Fourth Dynasty, and mother of Cheops, who built the Great Pyramid at Giza, is complete. It was discovered in a storage pit near the pyramid, and has since been reconstructed and put on show in the Cairo Museum. Reconstruction was made possible by the thick gold plating which sheathed nearly all the wooden elements.

Queen Hetepheres had an elegant armchair, a carrying-chair, a bed *11* of standard Egyptian type, with a footboard but no headboard, a headrest, and a large collapsible canopy which could be erected round the bed. This canopy, when folded, was stored in a long narrow box. There were also storage boxes for toilet articles and jewellery.

Many of Queen Hetepheres' possessions seem astonishingly modern, and even those features which appear to be alien – such as the custom of sleeping on a hard wooden headrest rather than a pillow –

can easily be paralleled elsewhere, not only in tribal Africa, but in China and Japan: anywhere, in fact, where it was more convenient not to disturb an elaborate hairdo.

The furniture discovered in the tomb of the boy-Pharaoh Tutankhamun (1361–1352 BC) is more than a thousand years later than that of Queen Hetepheres, but in many respects has a close resemblance to it, indicating the essential conservatism of Egyptian society. Tutankhamun's furniture does, however, present us with a much greater variety of forms and of techniques of decoration. There are a number of elaborate chairs. One, with arms, is a development of the Queen's; another repeats the same form, but is armless. A third, *1* the so-called 'ceremonial chair', is completely different. The base is like that of an X-shaped folding stool, and it supports a deeply curved seat, made of ebony and inlaid with irregular pieces of ivory to imitate goatskin. There is a separate panelled back – the panelling resembles the wall-decoration of contemporary buildings. The chair is accompanied by a matching footstool, inlaid with nine bound figures who represent the traditional enemies of Egypt. This chair exhibits many features which are familiar from the ceremonial furniture of later times. Points to note are the use of precious wood – the Egyptians prized ebony not only for its hardness and density of grain but because it had to be imported at great expense – and the method of decorating this wood by inlaying it with other substances. The decoration combines imitative and symbolic elements. For some reason, furniture-makers seem to take a particular delight in rendering one material in terms of another, just as they like to stress any ceremonial aspect by the use of appropriate symbolism. The bound prisoners lying beneath the king's feet on the royal footstool are an especially direct example.

Tutankhamun's funerary equipment also included both fixed and folding stools, a small three-legged stool or table, and about thirty chests of different types. These differed in size and form according to their intended function – small coffers were for jewellery, larger ones for bedding and household linen. The interiors of these boxes were often divided according to the specialized function they were meant to serve – the Egyptians were no strangers to 'fitted' furniture. Some of the coffers had domed or gabled lids, and one box was made in the shape of a royal cartouche. One oddity was the fact that very few were provided with drawers. The Egyptians had already grasped the principle of the drawer, but for some reason used it exclusively on small gaming- and toilet-boxes.

The beds found in the tomb are of the usual Egyptian form, well adapted to a hot climate because they permit the circulation of air round the body. They are lightly constructed, with resilient webbing or matting on a frame, a marked dip in the middle and a footboard but no headboard. Though chairs were already used ceremonially, beds apparently were not. The decoration on the footboard was for the pleasure of the occupant, not to impress those who looked at him. One of Tutankhamun's beds was made to fold for travelling – a precursor of the camp-beds of the Napoleonic period.

We know a good deal about Ancient Egyptian woodworking techniques. Coffins tell us that they knew a number of different sorts of joints: the plain butt joint, the mitre joint secured by dowels, shoulder-mitres and double shoulder-mitres, plus dovetails, dovetail-mitre-housings and halving joints. Most of these can be illustrated from coffins of the Old Kingdom period. The one common tool which the Egyptians seem to have lacked was the wood-turning lathe. The Roman writer Pliny the Elder credits this to the seventh century BC, and it may have been invented by either Syrians or Greeks. The Egyptian stool-legs that give the appearance of having been turned were probably hand-worked.

For information about Western Asiatic furniture, we have to rely not on actual specimens, but on the way in which the pieces are shown in works of art. These illustrations range from cylinder seals to large-scale Assyrian and Persian relief-carvings. These depictions may 12

12 Throne-chair and X-framed table on a Late Assyrian cylinder seal

13 Darius enthroned. Relief from the Treasury, Persepolis, sixth to fifth century BC

not give as much detail as we would like about materials and construction, but in compensation for this they often supply the social context in which a particular piece of furniture was used. We discover, for example, that the honorific function of the seat (the stool as well as the chair) was even more firmly stressed here than it was in Egypt. There are no equivalents for the convivial banquet scenes depicted in Egyptian tomb-paintings. One, from the Eighteenth Dynasty, shows a whole party of revellers, each of whom is seated upon a chair, while attendants bring garlands and pour drinks. In the art of Western Asia the seated figure is a king or a god; and those who stand are worshippers or attendants. The stiff magnificence of these

13   Oriental courts is well conveyed in a relief from Persepolis.

What we do find in this region, however, is that couches were now used in a different way – to lie on at dinner, as well as to sleep on. A

14   Neo-Assyrian bas-relief in the British Museum shows Assurbanipal (662–627 BC) feasting in the royal gardens, after defeating the King of Elam. Assurbanipal reclines on a high couch, with a table beside him, while his queen sits near by in an armchair, with her feet on a footstool. The defeated king's head hangs gruesomely in a tree.

This scene illustrates a pattern of behaviour which was transmitted to the Greeks, the Etruscans, and eventually to the Romans. Though

15   Etruscan terracotta sarcophagi show men and women reclining side by side, sharing the same couch, this was not the pattern in Greece, where convivial entertainments were very much a masculine affair. Women, if they were present, were servants, or professional entertainers, or perhaps courtesans.

20

14 Neo-Assyrian bas-relief. Assurbanipal and his wife feasting, sixth century BC

In the earliest Greek societies – or so it seems from the scanty evidence that survives – furniture was neither purely practical, nor purely ceremonial, but, as in Egypt, a bit of both. The throne discovered by Arthur Evans in the Palace at Knossos is all the more *16* impressive because we see it in its original context, as the focal point of the hall in which the king gave audience, flanked by his courtiers and counsellors, who sat on benches built against the sides of the room.

15 Terracotta sarcophagus. An Etruscan noble and his wife feasting

The throne has survived because it was made of stone, but it is evident from many of its details that it is a replica of something that was originally made of wood. Indeed, various wooden replicas have been made in modern times to show its probable construction, with a curved stretcher echoing the arch made by the two front legs, and straight, purely practical stretchers, joining the front legs to the back ones. The design, therefore, is not entirely harmonious, since the lines of the two kinds of stretchers conflict.

It is also possible to hazard a guess, though perhaps a less accurate one, at the construction of the chair upon which is seated the little
17 Cycladic harpist in Athens. The construction resembles that of the ceremonial chair of Tutankhamun, in that seat and back are almost dissociated from one another. This is a perfectly self-sufficient stool to which a back has afterwards been added.

The range of Greek furniture-types is not, in fact, very much larger than the range of Egyptian ones. In Greece, too, one finds chairs, stools, couches, chests, small tables and not much else. Though our knowledge of Greek furniture is derived almost entirely from vase-paintings and from sculpture, apparently accurate reconstructions have been made, a few at the end of the eighteenth and beginning of the nineteenth centuries, and quite a large number more recently by a firm in Athens.

Greek chairs can be split into two basic types. One is the heavy throne or seat of honour. Some of these derive directly from Egyptian and Western Asiatic prototypes, and they reached the height of impressiveness and elaboration in the thrones provided for cult statues in the temples. Nevertheless thrones could also form a part of private furnishings, at least among the wealthy. We find them in scenes of daily life painted on vases, and one is mentioned in an inventory of Alcibiades' belongings. Another, later type of throne – usually
18 Hellenistic or Roman in date – was placed in theatres for magistrates and other important people. Since they were outdoors, these thrones were made of marble, and have survived in some quantity. They usually have a rounded back and solid sides.

No form of throne, however, exercised such an enduring spell on posterity as the Greek *klismos* or light chair. Depicted in vase-paintings or reliefs, or as a reconstruction, it strikes us as something completely practical and contemporary. In Greek art, the *klismos* is a piece of furniture particularly associated with women, and its

22

16 The throne-room at the palace of Knossos, Crete, *c.* 1450 BC

17 Cycladic statuette of a seated
harpist, *c.* 3,000–2,000 BC

18 Seat of honour of the priest of
Dionysius Eleutherius, Theatre of
Dionysius, Athens

19 (*opposite*) Greek *klismos*.
Gravestone of Hegeso, National
Museum, Athens, *c.* 400 BC

20 Roman X-framed chair.
Detail from the *Sarcophagus of
the Seven Wise Men*, AD 250–60

ambiance is one of domestic comfort rather than ceremony. It seems
to be a purely Greek invention, and has no Egyptian or Asiatic
prototype.

The evolution of the *klismos* matched that of Greek art in general.
During the archaic period we see various experiments with the
proportions of the various elements, but by the fifth century these
were already standardized. As we see from the typical fifth-century
example represented on the gravestone of Hegeso, now in the   *19*
National Museum in Athens, the back of the chair and the back legs
formed a single continuous curve, while the front legs curved
forward proportionately in order to balance the sweep of the back
ones. The back itself was crowned by a deep, slightly curved
horizontal board, placed at shoulder height. This in turn was
supported, not only by the two uprights, but by a central splat.

In Hellenistic times the *klismos* became heavier, and its lines were
stiffer. Under the Romans, the design lost its popularity almost   *20*
completely. No other item of furniture now seems as completely
typical of Greek design as this beautifully proportioned type of chair.

Greek stools, like Greek chairs, follow two basic patterns. One has
four straight, usually turned, legs. The gods sit on stools of this kind in
one section of the Parthenon frieze, and it appears often in domestic

scenes in vase-paintings, nowhere more charmingly than in the little
tondo which shows a mother seated and facing her baby, who is
21 placed in a high chair which is itself evidently the work of a potter
rather than a carpenter, since it is basically a large bowl on a tall stand,
with holes cut for the infant's feet.

Another type of stool was the folding X-stool, already familiar
from Ancient Egyptian examples. One Greek author describes how
slave-attendants would carry these folding stools for their masters
when they went out 'so that, if they wished to sit down, they might
not be forced to put up with any chance seat'. The stools were often
supplied with animal legs ending in lion's paws, which faced inward.
One such is represented in the relief of a cat-and-dog fight, also in the
National Museum in Athens.

The Greek couch, which combined the functions of a bed and a
sofa, remained, like its Egyptian prototypes, a relatively light piece of
22 furniture. A vase-painting shows a young servant carrying one of
these couches on his back, with a small table placed on top of it. This
picture is also a reminder of the fact that Greek furniture probably had

26

21 (*opposite*) Mother seated on a stool, and child in a pottery high chair. Greek vase-painting, *c.* 400 BC

22 Servant carrying couch and table. From a vase by the Pan Painter, 475–450 BC

no fixed position in the domestic interior, but was brought out and moved around as needed. Greek couches differed from their Egyptian predecessors in two important respects: first, they stood higher off the ground, so much so that a footstool was sometimes used as a means of access; and second, there was now a headboard but no footboard. These changes were dictated by their use at banquets. Greater height made it easier to serve the food, and a backrest provided the diner with something to lean against.

The most typical kind of Greek table was small, portable, just low enough to be pushed away under a couch, and provided with three rather than four legs, which gave greater stability on uneven surfaces. The tables were used chiefly for eating (the Greeks hung their few possessions on the walls, rather than cluttering up the available flat surfaces), and were brought in or taken away, as required. In the fourth century the rectangular table gradually began to be replaced by one with a round top, and this came to predominate in Hellenistic times. Three-legged circular tables of this sort have had a long career since. They were particular favourites in the seventeenth and eighteenth centuries. Rustic examples were known as 'cricket' tables. Another, purely Hellenistic innovation was a table which consisted of a large rectangular slab, placed on two sturdy transverse supports. In ancient times these tables were usually made of marble, and were intended for outdoor use. The supports were often elaborately carved.

For storage the Greeks, like the Egyptians, used chests and boxes, though these are less often represented in art than other items, perhaps because their form was less interesting. An archaic terracotta plaque from Locri shows a woman opening a richly decorated chest to put in or take out a folded garment. Though some use was made of shelves (as opposed to simply hanging things on the wall), cupboards seem to have been unknown in the archaic and classical epochs. They were probably introduced in the Hellenistic age, and certainly appear in a number of Pompeian wall-paintings which seem to be based on Hellenistic Greek originals. One of their earliest uses may have been for the storage of books. Buffets for the display of plate and other valuable possessions may also have been a Hellenistic invention.

Roman furniture develops directly from Greek, though from late Republican times onwards it shows the typical Roman passion for luxury. Literary sources speak of the lavish use of precious woods, and of inlay in many different materials: gold, silver, copper, bronze, ivory and tortoise-shell. Some forms are typical of Roman rather than Greek art. One is a barrel-shaped tub chair which derives from a type popular among the Etruscans. In Roman art this is often shown in a purely domestic context, for example in a relief with three
23 philosophers debating, each seated comfortably in a chair of this type.
24 A real example carved from limestone was found in a tomb near Cologne and closely imitates a prototype made of plaited straw. Almost identical basket-seats are shown in late medieval miniatures illustrating scenes from peasant life, and they are to be found again in our own late twentieth-century domestic interiors – striking proof of the continuity of certain Western European furniture-types.

The form, however, must always be interpreted according to its context, as well as according to the shape and the actual material used. The barrel-shaped chair is to be found at its most authoritarian and
25 luxurious in the East Roman carved ivory throne which is now in Ravenna. This dates from the sixth century AD and accurately symbolizes the hierarchical society of that epoch.

28

23 Germano-Roman relief showing a school scene with men in tub chairs

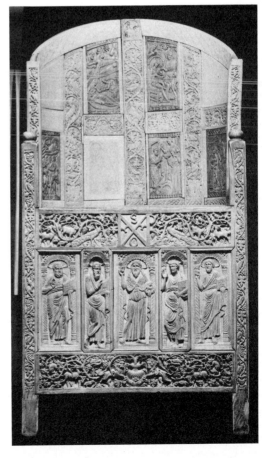

24 Limestone imitation of a wicker chair. From a Germano-Roman tomb

25 Ivory throne of Maximian, sixth century AD

26 Magistrate's *sella curulis*, from the grave-stele of C. Otacilius Oppianus, first century AD

27 (*opposite*) Circular bronze tripod-table from Pompeii, before 79 BC

Just as certain items of costume, originally items of everyday wear, came to symbolize formality or authority and were therefore considered appropriate for ceremonial or ritual occasions, so too perfectly ordinary items of furniture took on overtones which they did not originally possess. A case in point is the folding X-stool, which, as the *sella curulis*, came to be the emblem of the Roman magistrate's authority.

In Roman times the main impulse was towards ostentation. Couches, in particular, became a vehicle for lavish display. Particular care was lavished upon the fulcra against which the diners leaned. These were adorned with finely sculptured finials, usually in bronze. The subjects included heads of horses, mules and donkeys, and busts of maenads and satyrs (the two latter were considered especially appropriate because of their Dionysiac connections). During the later Roman period, couches began to be made with the addition of a back, like the modern sofa. An example appears in the interior of a sarcophagus found at Simpelveld, and now in Leiden. This

26

27

28

30

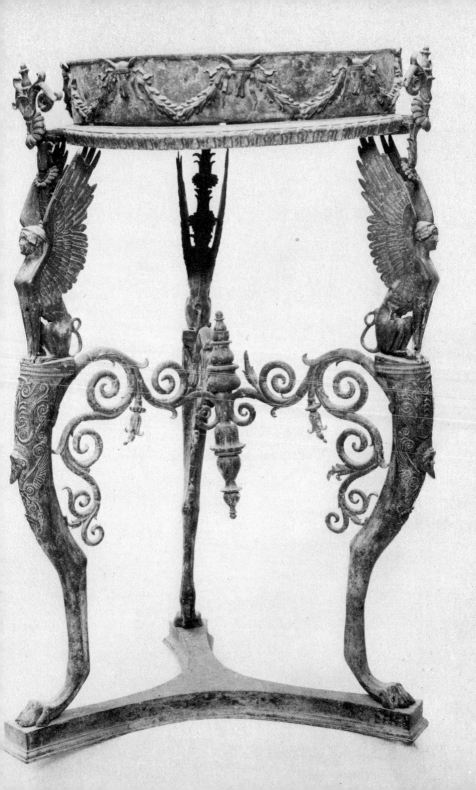

28 Romano–German sarcophagus from Simpelveld, showing house furnishings of the third century AD

sarcophagus also shows a Roman buffet, its shelves laden with vases and boxes, and also a semicircular console or side-table, made to be placed against a wall.

The rich differentiation of Roman furniture-types is eloquent of a settled and luxurious mode of existence. Some creature-comforts were still missing, however. Upholstered furniture was still unknown, though lavish use was made of cushions and pillows, and there were also richly coloured curtains and valances. Sometimes chairs and couches were completely shrouded in fitted loose covers. Representations of these covers occur in art from the late archaic period onwards.

Though furniture was occasionally used in a specific way to denote rank – the thrones of honour in Greek and Roman theatres are an instance of this – it was not, at least until the period of the Late Empire used in any very elaborately hierarchical way. The complex court ceremonies which came into vogue from the age of Diocletian onwards had a very definite influence on the history of medieval furniture. They were innovatory, but they also marked a reversion to customs and attitudes which had prevailed in the kingdoms of Western Asia.

CHAPTER THREE

The middle ages

We are much less well provided with information about furniture and the way it was used in the early middle ages than we are about its form and use in classical antiquity. Until the fourteenth century at least, actual specimens of furniture are exceedingly scarce; and even pictorial representations, most of them in manuscripts, and occasional sculptures offer relatively little information.

It seems clear that there was a considerable survival of Late Antique types. A leaf from a sixth-century consular diptych shows the central figure seated upon a throne which is not so very different from those occupied by Zeus on Greek coins and on Attic vases. It is notable, *29*

29 Late Antique throne. Leaf from the Diptych of Magas, AD 518

30 The Dagobert chair. Folding X-stool of Roman type with later back, seventh century AD

31 *The Dream of St Ursula* by Vittore Carpaccio. A luxurious Venetian interior of the late fifteenth century

however, that he is placed very high, with a tall footstool of two steps beneath his feet. An allusion is probably intended here to the description of Solomon's throne given in the Second Book of Chronicles. This was approached by no less than six steps, and was adorned with lions. Two lions' heads are visible supporting the throne on the ivory relief, and there are, in addition, curving legs which end in lion's paws.

34

32 *The Vision of St Augustine* by Carpaccio. Note the lectern and the shelf for books

Other seats of honour were less elaborate. In its original form, pre twelfth century, without the back and arms which were added later by Abbot Suger, the Dagobert chair, attributed to one of the French *30* Merovingian kings, was a folding stool with a close resemblance to the Roman *sella curulis*. In the Bayeux Tapestry, Edward the Confessor is shown seated upon another low stool, while his successor Harold has one to which a post-and-rail back has been added. Both of these look distinctly 'Roman'.

From the twelfth century onwards we have an increasing amount of information about medieval furniture, and this can take several forms: there are actual specimens, illustrations in works of art, and descriptive entries in inventories. Naturally this information refers chiefly to the furniture used by the upper class, but we may be reasonably certain that what the lower orders used was for the most part a simpler and rougher version of this.

Medieval kings and landowners were nomadic. It was easier to transport a great household to some new place, where food was available to feed its many members, than it was to bring the food itself

35

to a fixed centre. In addition, these peregrinations enabled the possessor to keep a personal eye on the administration of his lands. For this reason, furniture was either of the immensely solid and heavy variety which could safely be left in place when a particular dwelling was temporarily abandoned, or else made to be transported.

31, 32   'Fixed' furniture was often built in. Cupboards, for example, would be constructed within the thickness of a wall, and their emplacements are still often to be seen in medieval buildings, even when the woodwork itself has either perished or been destroyed. Seating could be constructed as part of the panelling of a room, and tables could also be fixed. In fact tables dormant, as they were called, are quite frequently referred to in medieval inventories. The fixed table could be so in one or both of two senses. First, the top could be fixed to the support – as we shall see, medieval tables more normally consisted of movable parts, trestles and the boards which were placed on top of them – and second these supports could themselves be fixed to the floor. In the hall at Winchester College there are five tables dormant fastened to the wooden floorboards; they are medieval in type, if not completely so in date (college records reveal extensive reworking and renewal in the sixteenth and seventeenth centuries).

Perhaps the commonest item of movable furniture in the middle ages was the chest, since it could be used both for transporting goods and for storing them once the destination was reached. However, there does seem to have been a broad division between these two functions, reflected by the creation of two different kinds of chest. One kind had feet and a flat lid, and was generally used for fixed

33, 38   storage. The other kind, used for transportation, had no feet, but a domed lid to throw off water. Sometimes a chest of the first sort would be provided with an outer covering, to protect it when it was being carried from one place to another; this covering was called the *bahut*, and might be made of tapestry, of wicker covered with leather, or even of wood. On occasion it was provided with locks of its own.

Locks could acquire a ritual as well as a practical importance, especially where some guild or corporation was involved. The common chest of the London Guildhall (*c.* 1427), which still survives, has no fewer than six locks, the keys to which were held by different officers. It was the custom to seal locks, so that the person who last had access to the contents of a particular chest would be readily identifiable by his personal seal.

36

33 Medieval Spanish iron-bound chest, reputed to have belonged to El Cid

The other common form of storage furniture was the cupboard or 7
armoire. Inventories tell us that these were often of fairly elaborate
character and were richly painted and gilded. Characteristically, the
painting and gilding cost far more than the actual structure of the
piece itself. Armoires could have special fittings to enable them to
serve particular functions. Some (there is at least one surviving
example) seem to have been equipped with rods or arms for hanging
clothes, and were thus the equivalent of the modern wardrobe. We
know less about these, however, than we do about another specialized
form of cupboard – those which were designed for the storage of
ecclesiastical or other records, sometimes being provided with a series
of small compartments; and sometimes, even, with drawers enclosed
within doors, like the surviving armoire of the Guild of Spanish
Merchants at Bruges (1441), now in the Gruuthuse Museum.

One thing that chests and cupboards had in common, in addition to
their function as storage, was the fact that they were purely practical,
and had little or nothing to do with expressing the gradations in the
medieval social hierarchy. Almost all other medieval furniture had
this double function. It was for use, and at the same time it served to
mark position within the pecking order. On this point I can do no
better than to quote from the introduction to Penelope Eames's
excellent specialist book on medieval furniture: 'The social
framework of society in which position, or *estate* as it was called, was
maintained and strengthened by visual means (the use of the correct

34 Charles V of France, seated under a sparver, being presented with a manuscript by Jean de Vaudetar, 1372

35 A fifteenth-century ceremonial scene, showing a five-stage buffet

"gear" in any situation being important), meant that certain objects, including certain kinds of furniture, were adjuncts of ceremony, subject to the rules of precedence, expressing in their character and form the degree of estate of a particular individual. The practical application of the rules governing the use of objects of estate was subtle, for the controlling consideration was *precedence* rather than *rank*. Precedence is mutable, changing according to the company of

39

any individual group of persons, whereas rank is a constant factor.' (Penelope Eames, *Medieval Furniture*, p. xix.)

Thus the peasant might sit in a chair at his own fireside, whereas at a feast in his lord's hall he would sit, if at all, on a bench at one of the tables below the dais.

The importance of the chair as a symbol of authority is relatively easy to understand, since it has survived until the present day. One essential factor was the presence of a footstool, or the placing of the seat of honour upon some kind of dais, and usually under a canopy as well. Medieval chairs of estate took several forms. Sometimes they were X-framed, in deference to the tradition inherited from the Roman world, as is the case with the Dagobert chair. Philippe I of France is shown on his seal of 1082 seated on an X-seat, and a miniature of 1372 shows Charles V of France using an X-framed chair in a more informal way, as he receives an illuminated Bible, though even here the notion of authority is emphasized by the presence of a conical canopy, or sparver, hanging over the King's head.

But there were also thrones constructed from planks. These were often elaborately decorated. The most celebrated surviving example is that upon which the kings and queens of England are still crowned: St Edward's chair in Westminster Abbey. Yet another method of construction is represented by the heavy armchair made of turned

36 Turned wood chair of estate reputed to have been used by King Stephen in 1138. Hereford Cathedral

37 Medieval Italian tavern scene showing octagonal table, three-legged stools and side-table

wood now in Hereford Cathedral, which was apparently made *c.*   *36*
1200. The fact that this was made as a chair of estate is confirmed by
the presence of a groove in the lowest rail at the front. This was clearly
made to link the chair with a matching footboard, which has now
been lost.

While chairs were supplied with loose cushions, as they had been in
classical times, there were also (according to surviving entries in
inventories) examples with upholstery. The accounts of Philip the
Bold, Duke of Burgundy, for the year 1390 speak of 'a chair, for the
Count of Nevers's inner chamber, of wood garnished with cloth and
padded with down and for a leather case in which the chair may be
placed.'

The commonest forms of seating, nevertheless, were not chairs, but
stools and benches, benches being in use particularly for dining.   *37, 39, 40*

The richly draped and canopied medieval bed is familiar not only
from paintings and illuminations, but from surviving examples,
though its supreme ceremonial importance has somewhat dropped
from view. It was preceded by a somewhat different and less elaborate

41

superbia

38 Late fifteenth-century Flemish interior, with narrow buffet, domed chest and table. Bosch, 'Pride' (detail from *Tabletop of the Seven Deadly Sins and the Four Last Things*)

39 Late fifteenth-century Flemish interior, with built-in bench, and chair with linenfold decoration. Bosch, 'Sloth' (detail as *38*)

43

40 Medieval feast, with narrow draped table on trestles. From a manuscript, *c.* 1400–05

type. This had short posts at each corner, standing perhaps fifteen inches above the mattress, and a low railing at each side which might be broken at one point to make the bed easier to enter. The canopy, if it existed at all, was a completely separate entity.

It was the thirteenth century that seems to have brought with it an increased emphasis on the importance of the canopy, and by the early

44

fourteenth century it had become absolutely necessary to any bed with seigneurial pretensions. The typical late medieval bed is fully draped, with a bedhead (tester or dorser) rising to a suspended canopy (celour). This in turn had curtains hanging from it, so that the occupant could draw these round himself or herself in order to enjoy additional warmth and privacy. The textiles used for these hung beds were vehicles for extravagantly luxurious display; the beds were regarded as heirlooms, and were often specifically mentioned in wills.

The canopy, which was the most important component in the

41 *The Death of Dick Whittington.* A fifteenth-century bed of estate with canopy

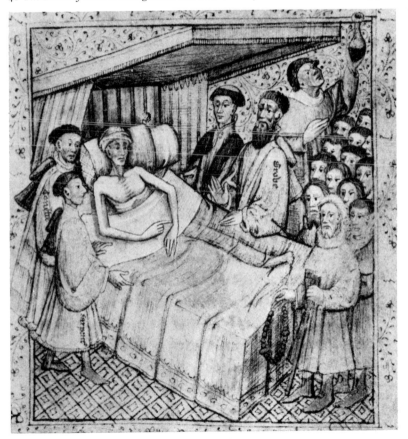

assemblage from the point of view of the honour it conferred, usually stretched the whole length of the bed, but occasionally demi-celours, 41 or half-canopies, were substituted. These were employed, for example, when several persons of rank occupied the same household, and served to mark the distinctions between them. Yet a third variety of canopy, sometimes used for beds, was the conical sparver, as can be seen over the chair of Charles V. This form seems to have been 34 especially fashionable in the fifteenth century, and it is mentioned in the inventories of Henry V and of the Count of Dunois, Joan of Arc's Bastard of Orleans.

By the fifteenth century hung beds had become so much part of the trappings of ceremony that they were often not intended to be slept in at all. When Charles the Bold, Duke of Burgundy, married Margaret of York in 1468, his apartment had a small room where he actually slept, and a reception room where he held state. This was furnished with what was called *un lit de parement*. The arrangement anticipates that found at Versailles in the eighteenth century. The rooms fitted up by Edward IV at Windsor in 1472 for the reception of Gruuthuse, the Burgundian Ambassador, had one bed for sleeping in and another, in a different part of the apartment, evidently just for show.

The great beds, with their celours, were sometimes matched by lesser beds, called couchettes, which often moved on wheels. At their most luxurious these were even provided with canopies of their own. For travelling, such couchettes were made with folding frames.

If beds played an important part in the ritual of medieval courtly etiquette, cradles too could be pressed into service. The rules concerning state cradles were exceedingly elaborate. We learn, for example, from Aliénor of Poitiers, author of the late fifteenth-century poem *Les Honneurs de la Cour*, that an infant of high rank must, on the day of its baptism, 'be brought into a chamber from the nursery and in that chamber there must be, as is customary, a high cradle hanging by means of iron rings between two wooden uprights. 47 The cradle must be provided with a circular or square pavilion [sparver] matching.'

The canopy must, Aliénor says, ideally be made of silk, a carpet should be laid before the cradle, and the baby itself covered with a counterpane of miniver (ermine).

This and other texts imply that the really grand baby was provided with two cradles, one for show and one for use, one for day and one

47

for night. The state cradle was high, and displayed the infant to the best advantage; the other was low, and could be rocked by someone sitting on a chair or stool. One may guess, however, that sometimes the night cradle was provided with both rockers and rings, so that it could be carried elsewhere and be suspended between uprights.

The other great vehicle for display, in addition to the hung bed, which aimed to stun the spectator with the extravagant sumptuosity of its stuffs, was the stepped buffet used for the display of plate. This, in its grandest form, might consist of as many as five or six shelves, arranged not one above the other, but like a staircase, and each loaded with objects in gold, silver and silver-gilt. Buffets of this kind were themselves of simple construction, since they were always draped with cloth when they were in use. The number of shelves used for the buffet was supposed to be connected with the rank of the person responsible for the display. A king or queen might show five or even six stages; a royal duchess four; a countess three, and so forth. The logical occasion for such a show of precious objects was a banquet or feast, but this was not invariably the case. A buffet might appear when a ruler was giving audience, as tangible evidence of his wealth, and therefore of his power.

One of the best descriptions we have of the function of the buffet, in terms of honour and its maintenance, concerns the Feast of the Pheasant, staged by Philip the Good, Duke of Burgundy, at Lille in 1454. On this occasion there was a six-staged buffet, close to the high table and surrounded by a railing, and only the cupbearers were allowed to approach it. At the feast of the Knights of the Golden Fleece two years later (another Burgundian court occasion), there were three buffets, the largest of which was of five or six stages. It was reserved solely for display, and was loaded with golden objects set with precious stones. The other two buffets, from which the tables were actually served, were filled with silver-gilt and plain silver plate respectively.

In addition to these stepped buffets of estate, there was another, smaller and more practical variety. Buffets of this type were the predecessors of the modern sideboard – they were used as a kind of half-way house for serving wine and other drinks, and also food, to persons seated near by at table. Many also had a place for storage, and another for display. These were not draped, and some were finely carved, especially upon the cupboard doors, and were adorned with iron hinges and strapwork, of the kind which appeared on good-quality armoires and chests.

Tables, the largest and most cumbersome items of medieval furniture next to beds, could, as we have already seen, be permanently fixed in place, but most often they were set up specially for meals, and when the meal was over were knocked down and taken away again. *37, 40* Meals were eaten where it seemed most convenient – sometimes in the great hall, but often elsewhere. At the time of the Gruuthuse embassy to Edward IV in 1472, Queen Elizabeth Woodville decided to entertain the Ambassador in her own quarters. The table was set up in the Queen's chamber, with a side table 'at which sat a great view of ladies, all on one side'. In an outer room was yet a third table, at which the Queen's ladies dined with the Ambassador's men.

Circular tables, both large and small, were also known. A remarkable survival is the huge circular table top, called King Arthur's Table but much later in date, which hangs on a wall at Winchester Castle. This is eighteen feet in diameter. Small circular tables could be supported by a single pedestal, quite in the classical manner, and some even had a screw in the pedestal, enabling the table top to be raised or lowered.

Though some late medieval furniture was of precious quality, and was lavishly adorned with painting, gilding and ornaments in precious metal, little of this has survived, and the survivors are chiefly small caskets. The rest often seems rather rough in workmanship. For this there were a variety of reasons. Medieval owners were interested in display; indeed display was actually one of the means whereby rich and powerful people asserted themselves. But, as the context was neither secure nor permanent, they spent money on things that were easily transportable and could be equally easily guarded.

Emphasis was placed, not on fine woodwork, but on luxurious hangings – silks and tapestries – and on objects made of precious metal. Rich stuffs had another advantage: they could be easily adapted to suit almost any context as the household moved to a new stopping-place. Even the rooms within a dwelling had not as yet acquired completely fixed functions, and this was one reason why furniture was thought to be of little account – it was moved in and out as required. This meant that it was either expected to survive the effects of fairly rough treatment or to be so essentially cheap and simple that rough treatment did not matter.

49

The strongest and best furniture was made of riven oak – the wood was made into planks by splitting the tree-trunk along the medullary rays from the circumference inwards to the centre, a technique borrowed from architecture and from shipbuilding. Exotic woods, of the kinds used by the Romans, were no longer available because of difficulties of transportation, and long-distance commerce confined itself to lighter and less bulky materials, such as rich silks. This was a subsidiary reason why textiles, rather than the furniture they covered, became one of the chief vehicles of extravagant display.

43 *St Jerome in his Study*. Elaborate Gothic library furniture from a Burgundian manuscript, *c.* 1410–16

The exceptions were churches and monasteries. Churches, because of their sacred character, had a better chance of protecting their property. Elaborate furniture formed a necessary part of a complete architectural ensemble dedicated to the glory of God. Choir-stalls, in particular, provided a vehicle for the skill of the medieval wood-carver, and show what he could have accomplished elsewhere if conditions had permitted him to do so.

Monasteries were even more important in the story of furniture because they were the first places, after the turmoil of the dark ages, to provide a framework for a tranquil and settled way of life. It is not therefore surprising that specialized furniture first developed in this context. Much of it seems to have been made for libraries, perhaps the first rooms to acquire a fixed identity of their own. Numerous late medieval depictions of St Jerome reading, usually with a lion at his *43* feet, undoubtedly represent an idealization of the scholar's existence. Despite this, they give a good idea of what the well-furnished medieval library was supposed to look like, and they show many highly specialized items of furniture: lecterns, cupboards, and places for displaying and storing books. Often they seem to be both finely made and elaborately decorated, and though they may to some extent be figments of the artist's imagination, it seems likely that he also had some actual models in mind.

Even more significant than the tranquillity provided by the great monasteries was the eventual growth of rich bourgeois trading communities in northern Italy and in Flanders. The interiors painted by the Flemish and Venetian masters of the fifteenth century have a new air of settled comfort. They show relatively small rooms in which the furniture seems to have not only a more or less fixed location but fixed functions as well. The style of this furniture remains Gothic, at least in the north (in Italy, classical details were already beginning to make their appearance), but there is far more emphasis on carved decoration, and less on rich fabrics. The cool, light-filled interiors depicted by Van Eyck, by the Master of Flémalle, and even on occasion by Hieronymus Bosch, already look forward to the *38, 39* ordered domestic scenes which were to be the delight of the great seventeenth-century Dutch genre painters such as Pieter de Hoogh and Jan Vermeer. They suggest, indeed, that something very similar *60* to the seventeenth-century bourgeois way of life had already begun to establish itself.

44 Tapestries at Hardwick Hall, Derbyshire

45 Typical sixteenth-century oak furniture in a reconstructed room from Sizergh Castle

CHAPTER FOUR

1500–1600

Sixteenth-century inventories present, on the whole, a surprisingly conventional picture of domestic furnishings and the way in which they were used. They demonstrate beyond contest, for example, that bedding and fabrics continued to be considered far more valuable than wooden furniture. The inventory taken at Hardwick Hall in Derbyshire in 1601, soon after the completion of Bess of Hardwick's magnificent country mansion, shows that tapestries were easily the *44* most spectacular part of the decoration. Hardwick has the reputation of being a series of almost intact late Elizabethan interiors. Records present a different picture. They show that, while many of the tapestries remain, often where they were originally hung, much furniture has been imported subsequently. The inventory does, however, enable us to identify some pieces of carved furniture as part of the original contents, and the fact that so few are listed suggests that they were, even at that period, still comparatively rare.

Indeed, sculptured and decorated furniture of quality, such as we *45* now automatically associate with sixteenth-century styles, seems to have been scarce throughout Europe, especially when compared to the number of upholstered pieces which, being more vulnerable, have not survived. The disparity of numbers emerges clearly from two important French inventories – that of the Connétable de Montmorency (1568) and that of Catherine de Médicis (1589). As one might expect, these list furniture of the most luxurious sort.

Further down the social scale, houses were, in modern terms, conspicuously underfurnished. An inventory taken at Oxford in the late sixteenth century proves, for instance, that there was very little furniture indeed in the house of a prosperous 'Doctor of Physicke', and that what there was consisted of the most basic items: beds, tables, stools, forms, chests, court-cupboards and the occasional chair. This inventory is typical.

Yet there was, nevertheless, a shift in taste which was taking place throughout Europe, greatly aided by the printing-press. Printing affected furniture-makers in two ways. One was through the dissemination of the theoretical texts which lay at the roots of the new renaissance classicism. From these texts developed, in turn, a new grammar of ornament – terms, caryatids, chimeras, columns and pilasters, laurel wreaths and palmettes. The development was aided not merely by illustrative engravings, but by knowledge of the surviving antique fragments on which these were based. In Italy such fragments lay close at hand. It was in northern Europe that the printed word and its accompanying illustrations had their greatest impact. It was a significant moment for the furniture-designer, for example, when the first text of Vitruvius to be published north of the Alps appeared at Strasbourg in 1543. In Germany there was a particularly strong response among makers and designers of furniture to classical theories of proportion, and apprentices in the furniture workshops

46 Architecture in little. A sixteenth-century German cabinet

47 Design for a cradle of estate
by Peter Flötner

were supposed to acquire at least the rudiments of these as part of
their professional training. By the end of the century, the two-tier
cupboard in particular had become a recognized vehicle in the   46
Germanic lands for renaissance ideas about proportion and ornament.
Some specimens, such as the cabinet dated 1587, by Clement Petel,
and now in the Rathaus, Welheim, are in every detail like miniature
renaissance palaces – far more correctly classical than the buildings
which were being erected simultaneously by German architects.

Even more precise stylistic guidance was given to furniture-makers
by the first printed pattern-books. Among the most important
designers were Peter Flötner in Germany, Jacques Androuet du   47
Cerceau I and Hugues Sambin in France, and Hans Vredeman de   53
Vries and Theodore de Bry in the Netherlands. Furniture still exists
which seems to be more or less directly taken from the ideas provided
by these designers, and in a more general sense their influence was
incalculably wide, and led to a distinct limitation of the master
craftsman's own creative freedom.

In northern Europe, the sixteenth century also saw important changes in the way in which furniture was actually constructed, and, as a result, there were also changes in the way in which the furniture trade itself was organized. Joined furniture – small panels in frames and uprights, pegged together – gave furniture a lighter and more movable character. Construction of this type also gave more play in damp climates, allowing the various parts to expand and contract without splitting. It did not develop to nearly the same extent in Italy and Spain because the practical necessity for it was less.

The joiners, who were the masters of the new techniques, were soon in conflict with the turners and carpenters, who used older methods. The struggle led to an elaboration of the guild system, with frontiers being drawn between qualifications and skills which had previously been lumped together. In Alsace, for example, there is evidence of a growing division between carpenters, now mostly employed on housebuilding, and joiners, which led to the formation of a new joiners' guild in 1519. With the need to define different sorts of skill precisely, guild ordinances became increasingly elaborate; and with increased consciousness of skill, guilds established themselves wherever European influence penetrated. On 30 August 1568, for example, ordinances for carpenters, sculptors, joiners and makers of stringed instruments were issued in the City of Mexico. One regulation forbade any craftsman to open a shop in the City without first being examined in his trade.

In Europe, the fact that the joiners were almost invariably triumphant in inter-guild conflicts helped to establish joinery as the standard method of making furniture – in England, for example, they had become recognized as the chief furniture-makers by the time of the accession of Queen Elizabeth I. But even within the joiner's trade there could be further divisions. In Amsterdam there was a guild of *witewerkers*, furniture-craftsmen allowed to use only white softwood. Though the furniture he made was meant to be painted, the *witewerker* was not allowed to do this part of the work himself.

Yet, despite rigid compartmentalization, there was still considerable movement of craftsmen from place to place, which led in turn to a blurring of stylistic boundaries. Sometimes craftsmen moved for economic reasons, sometimes because of political and economic conflicts. The growing prosperity of Amsterdam, as well as its significance as a place of refuge for Protestants, is symbolized by the

48 Joined furniture. Sixteenth-century English oak armchair with linenfold panels

fact that between 1500 and 1600 no less than 59 cabinet-makers and 12 chair-makers were incorporated into the Amsterdam woodworkers' guild. Many of these were immigrants from other parts of the Low Countries.

Immigrant craftsmen could introduce techniques and forms of construction that were not approved of by the local guild. In late sixteenth-century England, foreigners, mostly Flemings, began to reintroduce board construction as opposed to panel-set-in-frame. The new technique, with dovetails to fix the boards together to make a solid piece as wide as was wanted, was a vast improvement on medieval board construction. It enabled the craftsman to use rich and elaborate marquetry and veneers. Joined furniture, in these circumstances, began to look retrograde. The reign of joinery as the most advanced of furniture-making techniques lasted little more than a hundred years. But in one respect its influence was more durable. The methods that succeeded it – cabinet-making as distinct from joinery – often required the skills, not of one, but of several workmen. They also implied the existence of a prosperous and sophisticated clientele, willing to pay more for extra refinement. Joined furniture survived in small country workshops, and joinery became the typical idiom of the country craftsman. For the first time one begins to note the difference between metropolitan and rural furniture, not merely as a matter of quality, but also as a matter of actual technical approach to the problems involved.

Despite the dissemination of a new renaissance grammar of ornament, regional differences also became more marked in the sixteenth century than they had been earlier. For the first time we can talk of national styles in furniture.

In Italy, the seedbed of the renaissance, furniture was at its most classical. The true classical style is first seen there in mid fifteenth-century church furnishing, especially in Tuscany and Umbria, perhaps because the celebrated architects of the time exercised a strong influence over the way in which their church interiors were equipped. But domestic furniture soon began to show a close resemblance to contemporary ecclesiastical design. In fifteenth-century Florence we meet a good example of a truly regional type of
49 furniture. This was the *cassapanca*, a massive combined seat and chest. It was used in the main living apartment. Made comfortable with a mattress and soft cushions, it was the seat of ceremony for the master of the house. Closely related to the *cassapanca* was the *cassone*, but this was of more general distribution. The word, which means a chest, but with a nuance of importance and decorativeness, came into use only in the course of the fifteenth century. *Cassoni* were regarded as particularly suitable vehicles for decoration. In Florence, many were decorated with painted panels, some the work of the greatest masters of the time. Other forms of ornament for these chests were *pastiglia* work (a kind of low relief, gilded and occasionally painted), and
51 *intarsia*. *Intarsia* has a long history in Italy; it can be traced back to medieval times, when intricate stone inlay-work appeared in churches. In the renaissance *intarsia* workers enjoyed considerable fame; Giorgio Vasari wrote about them enthusiastically in his Lives of the artists, mentioning a number by name. Conservative Siena was especially famous for decoration of this type.

In the sixteenth century, however, carving became the favoured mode of ornament in Italy, just as it was elsewhere. From about the third decade of the century onwards, elaborately carved *cassoni*
50 appeared, shaped to resemble Roman sarcophagi. These demonstrate

58

49 Florentine renaissance
cassapanca, c. 1550

50 Italian walnut *cassone* of
the sixteenth century,
imitating a Roman
sarcophagus

51 Italian late sixteenth-century table of Roman form. Top inlaid with coloured
marble

52 Mid sixteenth-century Venetian folding chair in walnut

one of the ways in which the classical revival progressed. The craftsman found a model in Roman sarcophagi made of a different material, stone, and designed to serve a completely different purpose. Nevertheless, this satisfied him because it was stylistically 'correct', and he did not hesitate to translate it directly into his own medium. Another example of this process of translation is supplied by typical
51 renaissance centre-tables, with their massive supports in carved wood. These are versions of Roman garden tables in marble.

Italian furniture and modes of decoration were particularly influential in France and in Spain, though there was also a reciprocal current of influence from the Iberian peninsula after Italy began to fall under Habsburg domination following the Battle of Pavia (1525). But there were also developments which the French and the Spanish were not yet able to copy. One of these was the fact that in Italy furniture was no longer regularly carried from one habitation to another, but was allowed to remain where it was. This was partly because the Italian states were so small. Even when townspeople possessed country villas – and many fine ones were built in the

60

environs of Florence in the fifteenth and sixteenth centuries – they were for the most part content, while living in one house, to keep an eye on the other by means of occasional or even seasonal visits. This stability was a relatively new thing. Beatrice d'Este, when being received outside her husband Ludovico Sforza's Milanese dominions, mentions it as being a novelty when the hangings were not taken down as she vacated a particular apartment.

The town with the most luxurious life-style (though decorative styles, by contrast, remained for a long time conservatively Gothic) was undoubtedly Venice, protected against all comers by her lagoon. *52* Here a secure and stable domestic existence became possible from a very early date. Peter, the son of the King of Portugal, visiting Venice in 1425, wrote that the houses of the Venetian nobles who received him 'were not private houses, but palaces of kings and crowned heads'.

In France, Italian renaissance decorative styles were first introduced under Charles VIII and Francis I, as a direct result of the French invasions of Italy. Italian artisans, who supplied furniture as well as

53 French sixteenth-century walnut cabinet in the manner of Sambin

decorative features for the new palaces, were soon installed at Amboise and at Fontainebleau. Tables in particular showed strong evidence of Italian influence. They were not meant to be covered with a cloth as previously, and began to be made with elaborately carved feet. Because of the new interest in carving, oak, the favoured material for furniture in the French middle ages, was from about 1530 53 onwards replaced by walnut, which allowed for finer and more detailed work. Under Henry IV, influences from Spain, and more especially Flanders, were added to Italian ones. The furniture-industry grew rapidly, in step with the growth of the middle class. One sign of its growth was the fact that the turners achieved such importance that they were now installed in a special quarter of their own, part of the future Faubourg Saint-Antoine in Paris.

Yet despite all the decorative innovations of the Fontainebleau School, French attitudes towards furniture and its uses, especially in court circles, remained fundamentally conservative. So long as the court continued to base itself on the Loire, it remained nomadic. Each château was largely emptied of its contents as the court vacated it; and, using the same materials, a new environment was created elsewhere. The details of court ceremonial, which governed the way furniture was used, and sometimes even the forms it took, were those that had been inherited directly from the medieval past; many were to remain unchanged until the eighteenth century.

Spain accepted the new renaissance fashions from Italy only with some reluctance, and clung to many traditional ideas and customs of its own. Women, for instance, still tended to sit on cushions on the floor, after the Moorish fashion, rather than on chairs. Moorish influence remained conspicuous in the decoration of furniture, with intricate bone, ivory, ebony and boxwood geometric inlays in the 55 intricate *mudéjar* style, abstract in obedience to the tenets of Islam. These inlays reflected the Moorish habit of using very small bits of wood instead of a few larger ones, because of the scarcity of the material in the lands from which the Moors originally came. Spanish furniture, nevertheless, tended to be basically massive and unrefined in workmanship. It made frequent use of leather, especially for the 54 typical folding chair called a *sillón frailero*, and of massive iron hinges and iron braces for folding tables. These reflected not only Iberian tastes, but the materials and skills available, and the still-itinerant nature of aristocratic life despite the notoriously bad Spanish roads.

54 Sixteenth-century Spanish folding chair in walnut with original leather upholstery

55 Spanish sixteenth-century *vargueño* with *mudéjar*-style inlay in boxwood and ivory

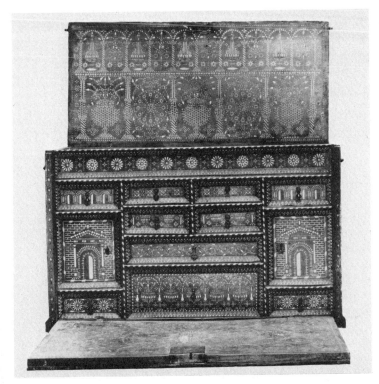

55   Just as the *cassapanca* is typical of Florence, so too the *vargueño* is typical of sixteenth-century Spain, though in fact the more elaborate specimens tend to date from early in the following century. The *vargueño* is a chest on a stand – or sometimes a chest on a chest – with a falling front, a development of the medieval hutch or treasure chest. The falling front, supported by runners which pull out from the stand, provides a surface upon which to write, just as drawers within the box give storage for papers as well as valuables. The *vargueño* is therefore the ancestor of the French eighteenth-century *secrétaire à abattant*.

Notwithstanding successive state bankruptcies, some Spanish sixteenth-century furniture was of considerable magnificence. Silver flowed in from the mines in the Indies, and its use in furniture became so well established that both Philip II and his successor had to bring in sumptuary laws (1593 and 1600) forbidding it. Sometimes it covered the whole piece, and sometimes an item would be solid silver. Antonio Pérez, Philip's one-time secretary and favourite, had beds, chairs, braziers, coffers and tables made of silver. One brazier alone was estimated to be worth 60,000 ducats.

Germany and Flanders also responded in their own fashion to the new stylistic currents. The high quality of some surviving German sixteenth-century furniture is a reminder of the fact that this region, despite its political fragmentation, and despite, too, the religious conflict, had become the centre of the European economic system, with a steady growth of population, a corresponding growth of towns, and the establishment of powerful corporations and craft guilds. Some of the best German sixteenth-century furniture was not princely, but was made for corporate clients.

In the Low Countries, as in Venice, a settled urban way of life tended to promote a recognizably modern attitude towards home furnishings. It seems almost an expression of this stability that furniture – beds as well as cupboards – was often built into the panelling of a room. The Dutch interior of the last decades of the century was probably more like the kind of home we might live in today than anything to be found in Italy, Spain and France.

England was stylistically the most eclectic and uncertain of all the regions discussed in this chapter. Renaissance ideas, in the reign of Henry VIII, were transmitted to England in an exceptionally pure and authentic form. But they did not really strike root. They remained no

64

56 'Romayne' work on an English oak chair, c. 1535

more than a court fashion, confined to an exceedingly small circle of aristocrats and intellectuals. Even later, when the renaissance achieved greater penetration, craftsmen used classical devices very crudely and superficially. A favourite ornamental device was a carved pseudo-classical head set in a panel, as an ornament on an otherwise 'vernacular' piece of joinery. These carved panels are referred to in contemporary sources as 'Romayne' work. But though in one sense 56 typical, they are really of little consequence to the stylistic development of English furniture as a whole. In fact the whole of the first half of the sixteenth century was noteworthy, not for any form of stylistic progress, but for practical improvements both in comfort and in furniture-making technique. There was a more widespread use of upholstered furniture, and an increase in the number of small movable pieces. In Elizabeth I's reign, certainly in the highest social circles, mere comfort occasionally gave place to rather flamboyant attempts at luxury. Marble-topped tables, for instance, were an

65

58 Sixteenth-century royalty at table. A banquet at the court of the Emperor Rudolph II

especially prized novelty. A number of these are reproduced in the Lumley Inventory, a fascinating pictorial record of the kind of 57 splendour a successful courtier might aspire to. It shows the possessions of John, Lord Lumley (?1534–1609). It was he who sold the house and park of Nonsuch to Elizabeth I in 1590. At this period, too, the custom had already been introduced of making whole suites of furniture covered in matching material. In 1581 Queen Elizabeth herself ordered a set of 19 chairs, 6 high stools, 24 square stools and 11 footstools, all upholstered in the same stuff.

By the end of the century a number of important innovations had occurred in European furniture. In particular, there had been some significant additions to the existing stock of furniture-types. The chest-of-drawers, for example, was introduced in Italy in the last decade of the sixteenth century. By the end of the century, the revolving chair had already become known in France.

Most interesting of all, from the point of view of the historian, were changes in form which reflected corresponding changes in social customs. Thus in the late sixteenth century, the tables people ate at became broader. The reason was quite simple. On non-ceremonial occasions, hosts and guests no longer sat on one side of the table only, with their backs to the wall. Now the host and hostess, instead of seating themselves in the middle, were placed at either end. These 58 alterations were in their own way more significant than the mere exchange of one decorative vocabulary for another.

67

57 (*opposite*) Luxurious Elizabethan furniture. A page from the Lumley Inventory, 1590

59 Furniture arrangement in the second half of the seventeenth century. The
North Drawing-room at Ham House, Surrey

CHAPTER FIVE

1600–1700

The furniture of the seventeenth century immediately seems more familiar to us than that of the sixteenth. There are more furniture-types whose use we immediately recognize – many, indeed, are still current today – and we get the feeling, when we look at well-preserved seventeenth-century interiors, such as those at Ham House   59 or at Skokloster in Sweden, that we are now moving into an epoch whose domestic manners are quite closely related to our own. There is, however, an element of illusion in this. The century, on closer inspection, turns out to be further removed from us than it seemed at first; and in any case it is difficult to characterize an epoch which is so deeply divided against itself.

I do not mean by this merely what is obvious – that in most countries there was a great step forward, in terms both of style and amenity. In Holland, it took place as early as 1625, when the solid oak cupboards of the sixteenth century began to be replaced by the flamboyant lacquer cabinets that Dutch traders were now bringing back from the Indies, or else by cabinets decorated with equally exotic ebony and tortoise-shell. In France and England, it happened somewhat later: in France with the accession of Louis XIV; in England with the Restoration of 1660 (though here some authorities would date it as much as twenty years earlier). Even Germany felt the change – there is a perceptible stylistic shift after the end of the Thirty Years War in 1648.

But there is also a division which persists throughout the whole epoch, the struggle between austerity on the one hand and unbridled flamboyance on the other. This contrast can be found in all the visual arts. In seventeenth-century painting, for example, the austerity of Georges de la Tour, Louis Le Nain and Zurbarán must be put beside the opulence of Rubens and Pietro da Cortona. Both qualities are equally typical of seventeenth-century sensibility. The interiors of the period can stun us with restless form and clashing colours, but they can also impress with their profound feeling for unostentatious order

60 Vermeer's *The Music Lesson*, a Dutch bourgeois interior, *c.* 1655

and regularity. This is nowhere better expressed than in the genre
60 scenes painted by Vermeer.

At this time ostentation remained to a large extent functional, just
as it had been in the middle ages. The glittering interiors at Versailles,
and their imitations elsewhere, were intended to impress beholders
with a sense of the wealth and power of those who had created them.
The silver furniture with which Louis XIV provided Versailles (the
main period of building lasted from 1661 to 1703) was as much a

visible capital reserve as the display of gold and silver plate on the buffet of a medieval ruler. It was melted down in the financial crisis at the end of the reign. Yet, even from the very beginning of the century, the hunger for comfort was beginning to grow. We find it expressed, for example, in the heavy upholstery of some of the early Stuart furniture now preserved at Knole. This arrived in the house via Frances Cranfield, daughter and sole heiress of Lionel Cranfield, Earl of Middlesex. Besides being a powerful minister and Master of the Great Wardrobe from 1618 to 1622, Cranfield was closely connected with the Mercers' Company, and we may be sure that these pieces represent the most advanced thinking of the time. Sofas and chairs are lower to the ground, and have deep cushions. The sofas have adjustable ends, and some of the chairs have adjustable backs.

The greatest influence for change, so far as the seventeenth-century interior was concerned, was undoubtedly the growth of trade. It was now possible to transport both finished articles of furniture and the raw materials for making furniture safely and economically to distant destinations. Now that some items were thought of as being precious in themselves, rich people, and more especially the passionate collectors among the rich, would go to some lengths to procure them. From the 1620s onwards English records show a certain amount of

61 Early Stuart luxury. An upholstered settee from Knole

furniture being imported from Venice for the court and for members of the nobility attached to it. In 1641, an inventory taken for the Countess of Arundel, wife of the collector-Earl, reveals that her household was provided with a number of pieces of furniture known to be of French and Italian origin. They included 'nine great Italian chairs of walnut-tree with arms, the seats and backs covered with red leather set with brass nails gilt'. Cardinal Mazarin's inventory, drawn up in 1653, lists twenty-two cabinets of ebony or tortoise-shell made in Germany, Italy and the Low Countries. He also owned Italian tables with marble tops encrusted with semi-precious stones.

One very significant new source of imported furniture was India and the adjacent lands. Indian craftsmen learned from Dutch, English and Portuguese colonists to make furniture which approximated to European forms. They also sent characteristic specimens of their own manufacture. Both were eagerly received. Towards the end of the century we find Sir Dudley North writing, in his influential *Considerations upon the East India Trade* (published in 1701, ten years after his death): 'The cheapest things are bought in India; as much labour or manufacture may be had there for two pence as in England for a shilling. The carriage there is dear, the customs are high, the merchant has great gains, and so has the retailer; yet still with all this charge, the Indians are a great deal cheaper than equal English manufacture.'

European manufacturers were soon inspired to try to imitate certain especially popular Indian techniques, since Indian goods, despite their cheapness, did not always precisely fulfil European needs, or fit in with European taste. One innovation for which India was responsible was the use of caning for the seats and backs of chairs. This was something lighter, more resilient and more durable than European alternatives. Convenient as they were, however, because of their lightness and comfort, cane-seated chairs tended to be despised because of their cheapness. They supply a rare example of upward social mobility in furniture, eventually finding their way into even the grandest and most splendid interiors. In England, large numbers were ordered under Charles II and James II for the official residences of the monarch – but they succeeded in penetrating the royal apartments themselves only under William III and Anne.

The other technique which had an especial impact on European furniture was that of lacquering or japanning. The splendid lacquer

chests and cabinets imported from India and further east soon inspired European imitations. In the 1614 inventory of the Earl of
Northampton we read of 'a large square Chinawork table and frame
of black varnish and gold', and there is also mention of 'one black field
bedstead painted with flowers and powdered with gold'. Imitation
lacquer is also known to have been made in Rome very early in the
seventeenth century. But the rage for this kind of decoration
continued to grow apace. In England towards the end of the century it
was greatly stimulated by the publication of an authoritative technical
manual, *A Treatise of Japanning and Varnishing* by John Stalker and
George Parker, which came out in 1688.

The craze for japanning was significant from the stylistic point of
view because the Oriental lacquer-workers supplied European
furniture-craftsmen with a whole new repertoire of exotic and quasi-
exotic designs. Painted furniture had, of course, been known in
Europe from the earliest times, but now it flaunted itself as part of
a new taste for the fantastic which was to have tremendous
consequences for interior design in the course of succeeding centuries.

Even more important than the importation into Europe of large
quantities of finished furniture, some of it from completely new
sources, was the trade in wood for furniture-making. There were in
fact two separate trades, especially so far as England was concerned.
Already, during the seventeenth century, English craftsmen began to
find there was a lack of native timbers suitable for their purposes. As a
result they began to import oak and fir-deal from Norway and the
Baltic, and walnut from Spain and France (some walnut also began to
come from the American colonies, especially Virginia). A constant
flow of supplies from overseas actually enabled English furniture-
makers to build up the beginnings of a reciprocal export trade in their
own products, already flourishing in late Stuart times. This was
eventually, in the eighteenth and nineteenth centuries, to make
England Europe's greatest furniture-exporter.

From the stylistic viewpoint, a significant development was the
growing trade in exotic hardwoods, particularly ebony. Ebony, with
its tremendous strength and hardness, was already known in Europe
in the middle ages (Marco Polo mentions it), and it seems first to have
been imported in significant quantity around 1500. Now it began to
flow into Europe from the East via the Dutch and English East India
trades. In England it was, according to surviving records, imported in

62 Imported Oriental cabinet on English carved wood stand, *c.* 1670

63 Cane-seated walnut chair made in England, *c.* 1690

64 Cabinet with ebony and
tortoise-shell inlay, made for
the French Crown, almost
certainly an early work by
Boulle (1642–1732)

such quantity that economic historians have sometimes been puzzled
to know how it was all used. Furniture-craftsmen used it chiefly for
making the elaborately decorated cabinets that had now become
fashionable. Here it was often used in conjunction with other rare and
64 exotic materials, which included ivory, tortoise-shell, brass, silver and
various semi-precious stones.

62 The cabinet, more particularly the cabinet on a stand, was as typical
of the seventeenth century as the carved buffet had been of the
sixteenth. No household of any pretensions was without one; and the
grandest, as evinced by Cardinal Mazarin's inventory, possessed a
great number. Though they could, of course, be used for storage,
their primary function was for show. Their development was closely

76

connected with the new rage for collecting which was sweeping Europe at the same period. The passion for collecting relics of the saints, which had obsessed some of the most powerful potentates of the late middle ages, was now replaced by more secular preoccupations, some of which had their roots in renaissance humanism, while others were more recent. Thus men collected coins and medals, women professed a passion for Oriental china, and both sexes took an interest in shells, mineral specimens and other natural curiosities.

From being repositories for these collectors' objects, cabinets became in some sense an actual framework for displaying them. An Englishman on the Grand Tour, such as John Evelyn, would commission a piece of furniture of this type as a framework for the 66
pietre dure or hardstone panels he had purchased in Florence, where the Grand Ducal workshops were famous for mosaic-work in semi-precious stones.

The intricate workmanship required in making these cabinets called for an entirely new degree of skill in furniture-manufacture. In France, where Queen Marie de Médicis is said to have been responsible for introducing the taste for ebony furniture, cabinet-making specialists became known as *ébénistes*. The first *maîtres ébénistes* are mentioned in Paris in 1638. Through a natural extension, it was these highly skilled men who also became associated with the making of all furniture which consisted of a solid carcass covered by intricately inlaid ornamental veneers, though the cabinet itself, being the showiest item they were called upon to make, remained the primary vehicle for their skill. They retained their popularity throughout the century. Out of a total of rather more than 500 pieces of furniture mentioned in the inventory of furniture belonging to the French Crown drawn up in 1700, no less than 76 are cabinets.

Another seventeenth-century innovation was the large mirror, architecturally used, and often with a marble-topped side-table 65
placed at the foot of it, both as a protective barrier and as a place to display decorative knick-knacks, often the Oriental china aforementioned. These mirrors were to be found in important houses all over Europe – since they were inordinately expensive, to possess them was a sign of wealth and prestige.

In some respects large mirrors and their accompanying console tables were even more of a milestone in the development of the

66 Cabinet with Florentine *pietre dure* panels made for John Evelyn

65 (*opposite*) Silver furniture from Knole in Charles II style

decorative arts than the introduction of cabinets made of exotic woods. There were several reasons for this. One was purely practical – these great reflecting sheets brought much more light into the rooms in which they were placed, and doubled and redoubled the power of lamps and candles at night. This made it possible to use enclosed space in a much freer way. If we look at Dutch genre scenes representing interiors, of a type which are usually either too early or too humble to contain large looking-glasses, we notice the habit of concentrating all domestic life as near to a window as possible. In the homes of the rich, the mirror mitigated this kind of constraint.

Large mirrors were important from more than a purely practical point of view, as it was this innovation that led to the creation of unified schemes of decoration on a large scale. The first fully integrated interiors were the small cabinets or studies created for renaissance princes in Italy. One such – not the earliest example by any means – is the *studiolo* in the Palazzo Vecchio in Florence. Such rooms were like very large pieces of furniture in themselves. The same can be said of the small private oratories made of inlaid wood which were sometimes made for Italian churches.

A different kind of integrated interior had elaborate painted decoration, like Raphael's *stanze* in the Vatican. But here the furniture was either irrelevant to, or even at odds with, what was painted on the walls.

The large mirror seemed to break through the wall upon which it was placed and at the same time offered an image of everything placed in front of it. It thus encouraged designers to integrate furniture and interior architecture in a way which had never previously been attempted. The furnishings, such as the console tables that were placed beneath the mirrors, were no longer allowed to make their statements in isolation. The table was linked directly, in form and ornamentation, to the frame that surrounded the mirror above; this frame, in turn, was linked to any other carved or painted decoration there might be on the walls, and the whole was reflected in other mirrors in the same room.

The mode originated in Italy, and specifically in Rome, which enjoyed a great revival of prosperity during the first half of the seventeenth century, under a series of vigorously nepotistic popes, many with a passion for building. The period saw the emergence of a number of extremely wealthy new families, their fortunes created by papal patronage. They expressed their exuberant sense of power and riches by building palaces in the prevailing baroque style. A good example of the type of interior favoured by these Roman patrons can be seen in the Palazzo Colonna in Rome, where splendid carved console tables under mirrors are supported by figures of Turkish slaves. It was largely from these Italian exemplars that the new French decorative mode under Louis XIV borrowed its most recognizable ingredients. The channel of transmission was Mazarin, an Italian who enjoyed supreme power in France.

But Louis could never be content merely to copy. The new integrated interior which expressed his sense of his own magnificence was also to be a way of encouraging French industries. In 1665, acting on his instructions, his minister Colbert established a mirror-glass factory in the Faubourg Saint-Antoine, which had been associated with the furniture trade since the reign of Henry IV. In 1688 this factory invented a method of casting sheets of glass of any required size, thus making possible the splendours of the Galerie des Glaces at   67
Versailles.

In another way, too, Louis and his ministers built on foundations Mazarin had already laid. Mazarin had loved fine furniture and had collected it systematically. Now a furniture-manufactory to supply the royal palaces was started at the Gobelins, and in 1667 its status was   68
raised to that of 'Manufacture Royale des Meubles de la Couronne'. Meanwhile in 1663 the French royal Garde-Meuble, which descended in its essentials from the middle ages, was reorganized into its definitive form. These two organizations supplied the King with the means to create the kind of surroundings he thought worthy of himself, and the painter Charles Le Brun served him as a kind of over-all commissar for the visual arts, though very much under his super-vision. The King's correspondence with Colbert demonstrates the minute attention he gave to matters of this sort.

Because of Louis' political and military success, and because, too, of his abilities as a propagandist, the whole of Europe tended to follow the lead thus offered. For example, in England, especially post-1660, the new high-backed upholstered chairs (themselves made possible by the fact that stiff ruffs had gone out of fashion) were referred to as 'French' chairs, and everything, as far as possible, conformed to the pattern set at Versailles. There was even a fashion for furniture made of silver, in direct rivalry with the splendours Louis had invented for   65

81

68 Louis XIV visiting the manufactory of the Gobelins. Tapestry from a cartoon by Charles Le Brun, c. 1666

himself. It is perhaps ironic that some English, though no French, specimens have survived.

Yet the French court could not dominate in everything, if only because it remained bound to some extent by its own traditions both of etiquette and organization. Even at the beginning of Louis XIV's reign, for example, the royal châteaux followed medieval tradition in being for the most part empty of furniture. When the court planned to visit a particular château the furnishings had to be transported especially from the Garde-Meuble in Paris. This situation did not change completely until the next century. The type of furniture employed at court was a mixture of novelties and survivals. For reasons of etiquette, stools – the *tabouret* and the *ployant* – were very numerous. With his strong sense of what was due to him, Louis XIV even made his ministers sit on humble *ployants* in the Cabinet du Conseil. 69

The Duc de Saint-Simon, whose memoirs are much concerned with points of etiquette, devotes a great deal of space to stools, and to who was and who was not allowed to sit on them in the royal

83

67 (*opposite*) The Galerie des Glaces, Versailles

69 The *Lotterie Royale*, Paris 1675. The three figures within the
square are seated on *ployants*

presence. In 1695, for example, he recounts how the wife whom he
had just married took her *tabouret* as a 'new' duchess at court: 'On
coming to table, the king said to her: "Madame, please be seated."
The king's serviette having been unfolded, he saw all the duchesses
and princesses still standing, and got up from his chair and said to
Mme de Saint-Simon: "Madame, I have already asked you to be
seated." Then all of those who had the right sat down, and Mme de
Saint-Simon between my mother and hers, who was after her.'

There was even such a thing as *un tabouret de grâce et pour une seule
fois*, the right to sit on a stool granted to someone who did not merit it
by rank, as an exceptional favour and for a single occasion only.

If such points remained important, the century also saw an
increasing rationalization of the uses to which various rooms were
put, but all the same this could sometimes take curious forms,
especially in the more exalted reaches of society. In palaces all over
Europe people lived in 'apartments', a series of rooms opening one
out of the other, railroad-car fashion. The last and principal room in
such a suite was the bedroom, with perhaps a small private closet off it,
for dressing or relieving oneself. It was therefore the bedroom that
remained, just as it had been in the middle ages, the chief focus for
social life, with guests crowded on stools round the great bed itself.
Saint-Simon describes how the widowed Duchesse d'Orléans, as late
as 1710, took to her bed as a matter of course, in order to receive
formal condolences on the death of her husband. Because the

70 A doll's house made in Nuremberg, 1639

73 bedroom had so much prestige, meals were often served there too. A
70 German doll's house dated 1639, a perfect replica of an important
mansion of that date, shows us a living-room with a large bed in one
corner and a dining-table in the centre.

Conservatism about habits of living did not prevent the
development of new furniture-types in answer to new needs. Some
examples have already been mentioned, such as the light and portable
63 cane chair, but there are a number of others. One is the sofa,
essentially an armchair extended laterally so that it would now seat
71 two or more people. Another is the glazed bookcase, which may have
been invented by that ardent bibliophile Samuel Pepys. An entry in
his diary for 15 October 1668 reminds us of the keen interest he took
in such domestic matters. It describes how he went to fetch 'Mr
Harrison, the upholsterer', and took him 'to take measure of Mr
Wren's bed at St James's, I being resolved to have just such another
made for me'. The seventeenth century saw a great increase in the
number of small pieces of furniture, tables, stands and the like, though
they were not as numerous as they were to become in the eighteenth
century.

71 Glazed bookcases
from the library of
Samuel Pepys

72 Marquetry writing-table made by Jensen for Kensington Palace, 1690. The turned supports are replacements

These small pieces represent an element of informality that had infiltrated what was still a very formal structure of living. Often they must have disrupted the grandiose decorative schemes of which the larger pieces of furniture in the same rooms formed an important part. One has a rather touching vision of people camping out amid their socially necessary but uncomfortable splendours, making themselves at home as best they could.

73 Seventeenth-century eating and sleeping arrangements, from an engraving by Abraham Bosse, *c.* 1635

Towards the end of the century, European furniture can be divided into three basic categories. Two of these were available only to the wealthy. One consisted of elaborately carved furniture which aspired towards the condition of sculpture, and which was also perhaps influenced by other crafts, such as silversmithing. Into this category 74 would fall things like the chairs carved in 1700 by the Venetian sculptor Andrea Brustolon for the Villa Pisani at Stra on the mainland. There are twelve chairs in the set, and they are intended to be emblematic of the months. Equally bold are the Dutch bases for console tables which look like enlargements of the work of the two Van Vianens, Paulus and Adam, perhaps the greatest Dutch silversmiths of the period. In these carved pieces we see the baroque tendency to develop a form three-dimensionally in space.

In complete contrast was high-quality veneered or cabinet furniture. In the last twenty years of the century this reached a pitch of refinement that was scarcely surpassed thereafter. Good examples are

the pieces made for William III and Mary II by Gerreit Jensen, who 72
worked for the English court from *c*. 1680 until his death in 1715.
Jensen's work is decorated with lacquer and seaweed marquetry, and
is sometimes fitted with mirror panels. As the seaweed marquetry
panels suggest, this is not furniture aiming at strongly three-
dimensional effects. It offers, instead, a refined and luxurious surface
to the sight and touch. Jensen represents the emergence of the master
cabinet-maker, who gathered together in his shop specialists in every
branch of the trade in order to supply as complete a service as possible
to his customers. It was in this direction that the more ambitious part
of the London furniture trade was to develop.

Finally, there was a large production of ordinary, utilitarian
furniture. Here the seventeenth century saw the emergence of certain
basic types which were to enjoy a remarkably long life. Many,
indeed, were refinements and simplifications of existing late
sixteenth-century models. Thus, for example, there is still a distinctly

74 Venetian sculptured armchair, by
Brustolon, 1700

late renaissance look to the plain table at which the saint sits reading in
76 Daniele Crespi's *St Charles Borromeo Fasting*, a painting which dates
from *c.* 1627–28. Such tables were to go on being made in Italy until
the mid nineteenth century. The tavern furniture one sees in pictures
75 by David Teniers II and Jan Steen is equally dateless, and is also almost
without nationality. Similar furniture was made both in England and
in her American colonies.

What seems to have happened is this. Certain pieces of furniture,
because of their essential practicality and usefulness, began during this
period to achieve definitive forms which they were to retain for many

75 Timeless furniture, Holland. A tavern scene by Steen, *c.* 1660

76 Timeless furniture, Italy. Detail from *St Charles Borromeo Fasting* by Crespi

years. Skilled but unsophisticated country craftsmen, usually joiners rather than cabinet-makers, repeated the same designs again and again, without changing them much, because they had been found to be the best for a particular purpose. A good deal of furniture thus escaped from the influence of fashion and, however unconsciously, responded only to the principle of fitness for use.

It was furniture of this type which eventually attracted the attention of nineteenth-century reformers such as William Morris, and which, through him, became the progenitor of a great many of the utilitarian modern designs which furnish people's houses today.

77 The Duc de Choiseul's study. Miniature on a snuffbox
by Van Blarenberghe

78 Comfort and informality under Louis XV. *A Reading from Molière* by de Troy

CHAPTER SIX

1700–1800

Eighteenth-century furniture is still *par excellence* the ideal of those who interest themselves in 'antiques'. They feel that what was made at this period corresponds to modern necessities while at the same time reflecting standards of elegance which the modern furniture-designer finds it difficult to achieve. This attitude perpetuates a subtle misunderstanding of eighteenth-century manners and society.

It is of course true to say that it was in this century that furniture-makers evolved a whole repertoire of specialist furniture-types, many of which are still current today. It is also true to say that for the first time one finds a real understanding of comfort as well as of luxury. There is a charming story about Mme Elisabeth, one of the spinster daughters of Louis XV, being asked why she had not entered a convent like her sister Mme Louise. 'C'est un fauteuil qui me perd', she replied: 'It was an armchair that was my undoing.' And, indeed, if one looks at some of the surviving low padded chairs of the mid century, or better still at a contemporary genre scene which shows them in use, such as Jean François de Troy's *A Reading from Molière*, it   78 is clear that there was not only a new feeling for comfort but a less self-conscious attitude to the human body, which was now, at least on more intimate occasions, allowed to relax from the stiff postures politeness had required earlier. Such furniture gives one a keen sense of that *douceur de vivre* which Talleyrand sighed for after the tempest of the French Revolution.

The kind of evidence I have just mentioned is not the only kind available. Much of the rest seems to point in a very different direction. Many English, as opposed to French, conversation-pieces show rooms which are surprisingly sparsely furnished, and in which the furniture itself is arranged in an unfamiliar and unsympathetic way – the chairs, for example, are often pushed back against the walls in   79 rigid rows. These pictures cover quite a range; they show us both ambitious and relatively unambitious interiors. Surviving documentation, which relates chiefly to the very grandest establishments,

93

confirms that these rigid arrangements were a matter of taste, and, even more, of accepted convention. A French snuff-box is decorated on all sides with minutely detailed miniatures by Louis-Nicolas van Blarenberghe, showing interiors of the Hôtel de Choiseul, town house of Louis XV's celebrated minister, the Duc de Choiseul. These demonstrate clearly the difference between what were called *chaises courantes* and *chaises meublantes*, as this is explained, for example, in the *Dictionnaire critique et raisonné des étiquettes de la Cour*, by Mme de Genlis. *Chaises courantes* stood in the centre of the room, ready for use, and could be moved about at will; *chaises meublantes* were meant to be left in position against the dado. Adam envisaged precisely the same arrangement in some of the state rooms at Osterley, when he redecorated the house for the Child family who were not aristocrats but rich bankers.

Yet while the prosperous class accepted the dictates of conventional etiquette, they were also becoming increasingly conscious of the discomforts this imposed on them. When Philip Yorke went to visit the Duke of Devonshire at Chatsworth in 1763, for example, he complained that the rooms of the state apartment were highly inconvenient, and 'of little use but to be walked through'. From the fifteenth century onwards people had had small closets and retiring rooms where they could hope for a little comfort and privacy. Now, where the money was available, they began to create complete duplicate suites of apartments – one set for show, and the other for use. The most famous example is the creation, under Louis XV, of the hidden *petits appartements* at Versailles, which enabled the King and his intimates to get away from the formality of the court. A similar arrangement exists in some of the great English country houses built between 1700 and 1800. Both Kedleston and Holkham have separate private wings for family living. Even where the separation was not quite so complete, it was customary to have a set of state rooms on the main floor (usually one floor above ground-level), while ordinary life went on above and below. In these state rooms, monuments to conspicuous consumption, the fine furnishings and even the rich curtains and carpets would normally be protected with fitted dustcovers – one reason why so much expensive upholstery has survived until the present day.

Within an apparently rigid physical and social structure there was, nevertheless, a place for improvization. Descriptions of life at

94

79 Mid eighteenth-century English furniture arrangement. A family group by Philip Hussey

Osterley suggest that, particularly in the Long Gallery, the lighter 5
furniture was freely moved about, placed where it was wanted, then
carefully replaced or removed by servants once the room was
unoccupied. French eighteenth-century prints with gallant and
sentimental subjects show interiors which exhibit a charming
disorder, in keeping with the dramas which are being enacted. But
one must imagine not a perpetually slovenly way of living, but a
legion of unseen helpers ready to set all to rights. If furniture was
mobile, rooms too remained flexible in their functions. As late as 1755
Mrs Delany writes of 'my "dining-room", vulgarly so called',
implying that it was in her view an innovation to have a room
specially set aside for eating. The word 'dining-room' does, however,
make its appearance in Dr Johnson's *Dictionary*, which was published

95

the same year. The big dining-table with removable sections or leaves became fashionable in England only as late as 1780 – before this it had been the custom to dine at several smaller tables. With the appearance of these big tables the function of the dining-room at last became fixed, as it was impossible to use the space for any other purpose.

With the growth of the middle class, more and more people were able to own good furniture. Daniel Defoe, describing a London fire which took place in 1713, says that the goods then taken out of a shopkeeper's house were 'far better than any removed at the late fire at the French ambassador's'. In France, things went forward a little more slowly, but by the reign of Louis XVI, a larger, distinctly bourgeois clientele was making its influence felt. Some shopkeepers were willing to cater even to the very poorest. Many eighteenth-century Londoners, for example, were forced to live in rooms as weekly tenants, in order to be near their place of work. Landlords often preferred not to provide furniture in these lodgings in case the tenants absconded with it. It was therefore possible to buy furniture on a hire-purchase system, at so much a week.

Among the rich, particularly in France, taste was an obsession and collecting fine furniture could become a kind of mania. One aristocratic lady, the Marquise de Massiac, was reputed to own fine furniture worth 2,000,000 livres. Mme de Pompadour, Louis XV's mistress, was said to have asked the King to give the *ébéniste* Migeon a pension of 3,000 livres per year because he made her a particularly convenient and beautiful close-stool. The French monarchs paid enormous sums for important items. The sumptuous chest-of-drawers made by Riesener for Louis XVI's bedroom at Versailles cost 25,356 livres. It took no less than fourteen months to complete, and at the time of the Revolution (1792) was still valued at 12,000 livres.

The obsession with taste and fashion brought with it a number of things that combined to give the furniture of the period a very particular character. Perhaps the most notable was the rapid turnover of styles; and these styles were sharply differentiated from one another, though more so in England than in France. Three groups of people profited from the public's desire for change. These were the merchants who sold furniture, the designers of ornament and publishers of pattern-books, and the established architects. These various groups collaborated with one another, and to some extent their functions overlapped.

80, 81

96

80, 81 Design by the Frères Slodtz, and commode made after it by Antoine Gaudreaux, with ormolu mounts by Jean-Jacques Caffiéri. c. 1739

The two main centres of diffusion for stylistic ideas were undoubtedly England and France, with the latter perhaps somewhat in the lead, particularly during the first half of the century. It is interesting to note how much they differed from one another.

One important difference was that in France the development of fashion was an organic thing, while in England it is easier to isolate the role of individuals. In France, luxury furniture was very conspicuously the result of a collaboration between a number of very different crafts. Because of the French habit of mounting important pieces in ormolu or gilded bronze, and of using lacquer and porcelain, the spectrum of these crafts was even wider in Paris than it was in *83, 82*

97

82 Cabinet on stand mounted with Sèvres porcelain plaques. Louis XVI. Signed Weisweiler

83 Lacquer commode mounted in ormolu. Louis XV. Signed B.V.R.B.

London, and the divisions between them were in any case more marked. Coordination began, not with an entire decorative scheme, but with a single piece of furniture. *Ebénistes* were purely cabinet-makers, but the frameworks to which they applied their intricate veneers, the *châssis* as they were called, might well be supplied by someone else. *Menuisiers*, who made chairs and anything carved, such as mirror frames and bases for console tables, belonged to a different guild altogether. As chair-makers, they collaborated with another professional group, that of the upholsterers.

The activities of the various craft-specialists could be directed in several different ways. Architects obviously exercised a certain amount of influence over what was to go into the interiors they designed, but they do not seem to have concerned themselves nearly as closely with furniture-design as architects in England, though an important piece of furniture would often be made for a predetermined position in a room, and would match its decoration. There are, nevertheless, no real French equivalents for Kent and Adam. Their place was to some extent taken by the *ornemanistes*, or makers of designs for ornament, though their suggestions for what a piece of furniture should look like were often greatly modified in the making – much more so than the designs Adam gave to craftsmen in England.

95

Where royal commissions were concerned, the responsibility for coordinating the efforts of the various craftsmen involved rested with the Superintendent of the royal Garde-Meuble. It was he, for instance, who saw to it that the products of the *ébéniste* and the *menuisier* were in harmony with one another.

Soon, as the century advanced, this function tended more and more to be taken over by the *marchand mercier*. The *marchands merciers* were traders in exotic material of all kinds. It was they, for example, who had been responsible for importing the lacquer cabinets so fashionable during the seventeenth century. Now their function expanded. It was probably the fact that they dealt in lacquer that brought them into direct contact with the leading furniture-workshops, as the idea soon arose of taking apart Japanese and Chinese cabinets and Coromandel screens, cutting and reshaping the panels wherever necessary, then using these to make pieces of furniture in European form. Some of the leading Parisian *ébénistes* became immensely skilful in using the rather intractable raw material which the *marchands merciers* provided. They even learned how to steam and shape the Oriental lacquer panels to make the swelling 83 (*bombé*) forms and sinuous curves required by rococo taste.

Once in contact with the actual furniture-makers, the *marchands merciers* became ever more ingenious and ambitious in the novelties they proposed to their customers. It was they, for example, who had 82 the idea of using Sèvres porcelain plaques for the decoration of furniture – a short step from mounting porcelain figures and vases in gilt bronze which had long been a speciality of theirs. The time eventually came when a proportion of royal commands went to these intermediaries, instead of via the Garde-Meuble directly to the furniture-makers, and when certain well-known *ébénistes* – Martin 83, 97 Carlin, B.V.R.B. and Adam Weisweiler, for example – worked for them almost exclusively.

The result of this system of patronage was that fashion, certainly during the first half of the century, moved forward continuously, but without decisive gaps or breaks between one fashion and another. Even the upheaval represented by neo-classicism was not quite so violent in France as it was in England. It is true that in the France of 1750 there were already protests against the extravagance of the rococo. There was also a nostalgia for the great days of Louis XIV, which led to a revival of interest in the rich late baroque furniture 64 made by André-Charles Boulle. But coherent neo-classical ensembles were not created in France until about 1770, and even then they rarely had the doctrinaire quality which neo-classicism rapidly acquired in England. It is one of the ironies of history that neo-classicism, consciously moral and anti-frivolous, found one of its first French promoters in the Marquis de Marigny, the Marquise de Pompadour's brother, and came fully into the public view with the inauguration, in 1770, of the luxurious pavilion at Louveciennes, owned by Mme du Barry, Mme de Pompadour's successor in the King's affections.

French rococo was hugely influential all over Europe during the first half of the century, and made especially characteristic appearances in Germany and in Italy. It did not, however, cross the frontiers of France without undergoing some degree of transformation. For example, the rococo interior designed as a whole, created under the direct control and supervision of a single individual, is much better seen in Germany than it is in its place of origin. The supreme exponent of the rococo style in Bavaria, where it perhaps

84 (*opposite*) Integrated decoration. The Reichen Zimmer at the Residenz, Munich, designed by Cuvilliés

reached its apogee, was the French-trained and French-descended
84 François Cuvilliés. The rooms designed by him for the Munich
Residenz, and still more so his designs for the Amalienburg pavilion,
show complete integration between the furniture and the interior
decoration. The elaborate designs on the walls flow over the case-
furniture and consoles placed against them without interruption, and
with very little acknowledgment of the demands of practical use.
Similarly integrated interiors were created for Frederick the Great at
Potsdam by the brothers Hoppenhaupt.

In Italy, and particularly in Venice, the rococo style took on a
distinctly theatrical air, in keeping with the carnival spirit of the place.
Quality was consistently sacrificed to effect. Venetian lacquer
85 furniture of the eighteenth century is delightfully colourful and
imaginative, but usually very roughly made, at the opposite pole
from French fastidiousness in such matters.

The interest felt in France in the single superb piece of furniture,
often taking relatively little account of its intended setting, operated

85 Venetian lacquer cabinet. Mid
eighteenth century

86 Marquetry *coiffeuse* made by Abraham Roentgen, father of David, in 1769 for Friedrich Augustus III, Elector of Saxony

in favour of at least one German cabinet-maker, who eventually became famous throughout Europe for his ingenious mechanical furniture. This was David Roentgen of Neuwied. Roentgen was so successful in the French market (the way had been prepared for him by the existence of other cabinet-makers of German origin, such as *86* Jean-François Oeben and Weisweiler) that at one time he had a subsidiary establishment in the French capital. In 1779 he was created *ébéniste-mécanicien du Roi et de la Reine*, a completely new post which marked his special status.

In England, the situation was in many respects different. The major influences on the development of furniture were: first, a handful of celebrated architects; second, a small group of dilettante patrons;

88 third, a well-integrated furniture trade, influenced by widely circulated pattern-books and catering not to the aristocracy alone but to the middle class. Stylistic progress was not smoothly continuous, but proceeded in a series of sudden leaps. In addition to this, there was an adumbration of the early nineteenth-century tendency for several quite distinct styles to exist simultaneously, without any one of them becoming dominant.

The first fully integrated interiors created in England were designed by the Palladian architect Kent. He was an important member of the circle which clustered round the Earl of Burlington, himself a talented architect. Burlington and his colleagues were trying to revive the achievements of Inigo Jones, the great architect of Charles I's time, who in turn had based his work on the achievements of the sixteenth-century Venetian, Andrea Palladio. Jones, and indeed Palladio himself, had left these eighteenth-century followers of their doctrines little guidance where furniture was concerned, but there was a general feeling that furniture ought somehow to match the interior which contained it. Kent's solution was to take the 87 architectural forms typical of Palladio and scale them down. The results were rich, florid and monumental. They were also extremely sparse. We are told that 'six or eight chairs and a couple of tables' were considered quite enough to furnish a room 'large enough to receive a company of sixty or one hundred persons'.

Kent's Palladianism was only one element in a battle of styles which continued intermittently throughout the century. Other possible choices were the so-called 'French' style (a version of rococo often very unlike that to be discovered in France), the Chinese and the Gothic. The two latter can also be regarded as having rococo associations.

Some pseudo-French furniture made in England did come fairly close to the original model. This is true of the fine commodes created 89 by the French émigré craftsman Pierre Langlois, with their bombé outlines. But even here the restraint of the decoration proclaims them to be the product of a different milieu. Far more typical of the effects of the rococo in England are the chair designs proposed by Thomas Chippendale in his Director, and produced by him and other leading London makers. What strikes one about these chairs is their linearity. 91 The fact that they were made of mahogany, not of beech (which was the usual material for chairs in France until very late in the century),

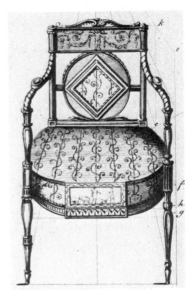

87 Carved giltwood stands after a design by Kent

88 Design by Sheraton for a drawing-room chair

89 Commode attributed to Langlois

90 Windsor chair with Gothic back. English, eighteenth century

91 Chippendale-style mahogany side-chair with ribbon splat

enabled the makers to indulge in pierced openwork carving of great virtuosity. This carving might, for example, represent a fluttering knot of ribbons; it might also, with little change in the basic outline of the chair, be turned into some kind of Gothic or Chinese fret.

90

The passion for the Gothic and the Chinese can be seen, in one sense, as a way of avoiding the implications of rococo freedom. Rococo forms were essentially created *de novo* – indeed, their claim to absolute novelty was, on the Continent at least, a major part of their attraction. The conservative English preferred to innovate by basing themselves on some historical or exotic precedent: the Palladian revival was a perfect example.

92

The Chinese fashion was less peculiarly English than the Gothic, since it had raged all over Europe during the previous century. In England a renewed enthusiasm for things Chinese was marked by a revival in the craft of japanning (the European imitation of Oriental

92 Bedstead in Chinese taste, probably made by Chippendale for the Fourth Duke of Beaufort, *c.* 1754

lacquer), which fell out of favour in about 1730 only to be taken up again in about 1750. By 1753 a writer in *The World* (a newspaper of the time) was able to assert that everything was now 'Chinese or in the Chinese taste'. The fashion was given a kind of consecration when Sir William Chambers published his *Designs for Chinese Buildings, Furniture, Dress, etc.* in 1757, but soon began to meet with opposition from neo-classicism. Nevertheless it survived in sufficient strength to inspire, at the beginning of the next century, the extravagant chinoiserie of the architecture and decoration of the Prince Regent's Royal Pavilion at Brighton.

93 *The Music Room* by John Nash, 1822. An Oriental interior at the Royal Pavilion, Brighton

91 Though Gothic had distinctly rococo overtones in the hands of designers such as Chippendale, it always took itself more seriously than the Chinese style. There were a number of reasons for this. One was that the Gothic itself had never completely died out in England, but still survived in attenuated form in the hands of provincial builders, and even in some of the work done in various Oxford colleges, until intellectuals and connoisseurs such as Walpole came along to take an interest in it. Walpole, despite the fact that he referred 94 to his beloved Strawberry Hill as a 'plaything house', put much research, energy and thought into his activities as a builder and decorator. Strawberry Hill was an extremely significant creation. It was not merely an essay in the Gothic but an attempt to bring a fantasy to life and to create an environment that reflected the personality of its owner in a new and original way. For Walpole, his house was a mirror which reflected the quirks of his own personality.

108

94 The Holbein Chamber, Strawberry Hill, Middlesex

This characteristic was to be carried much further in another and even more fantastic neo-Gothic creation: Beckford's Fonthill, which, despite its vast size, was designed as a setting for a recluse. For the first time, purely literary and subjective elements were triumphant in interior decoration and in the choice of furnishings. The battle between the rational and irrational elements – what one may describe as design for use as opposed to design for aesthetic, spiritual and even moral satisfaction – was thenceforth to characterize the development of European furniture.

The 'moral' element is particularly conspicuous in the development of neo-classicism. Neo-classicism was always strongly didactic in intention, and its originators aimed at the purification of society as well as art. Outside France it was also an expression of hostility to French cultural dominion which had prevailed since the reign of Louis XIV. In England, the most important architect-designer

95 Adam's designs for the dining-room furniture at Osterley. From his *Works in Architecture*, 1773

connected with the early phases of the neo-classical movement was
95 Adam, who exercised as total a control over the interiors he designed
as Cuvilliés had done earlier in Germany. Adam was by no means
opposed to certain aspects of French taste, as is demonstrated by his
use of specially woven sets of Gobelins tapestries at Osterley and
elsewhere. But essentially he was moving in a direction which must
ultimately destroy the rococo, while seeming to pay service to some
of its ideas about cheerfulness, lightness, elegance and novelty. By
1767, somewhat ahead of his contemporaries in France, he had
become thoroughly fluent in inventing neo-classical designs for
furniture.

Adam did not pretend, as later exponents of neo-classicism were to
do, that he was re-creating the kind of interiors Ancient Greeks or
Romans would have lived in. His aim, rather, was to draw on his
experience of Roman architecture and decoration – he was

particularly attracted by the stuccos and paintings in Nero's Domus Aurea in Rome and by some of the details he observed in Diocletian's palace at Spalato (Split) – in order to create interiors suitable for the senatorial Romans of another and more developed age, which was the way in which his classically educated English clients tended to think of themselves. He was extremely fortunate in his collaborators.

Chippendale's reputation as a craftsman must surely rest, not on anything he made in one of the variants of the English rococo style, but upon the inlaid furniture he made for Adam. This is as technically refined as anything produced in Roentgen's Neuwied workshops, but more restrained in design and better proportioned.

96

Chippendale's importance lies not merely in his influence as a rococo designer, nor in his collaboration with Adam, but in his role as the most visible of the links between leading English designers and the English furniture-industry. Chippendale's business, like Jensen's in the seventeenth century, was far more than just a workshop. He supplied customers not only with furniture, but with wallpapers and borders, curtains and blinds, in fact with almost everything necessary to furnish a house.

As far as the actual making of furniture was concerned, English arrangements were often rather different from French ones. There were some shops which, like the *marchands merciers* in Paris, took their

96 Desk in Adam style made for Harewood House, Yorkshire, *c.* 1770. Probably by Chippendale

stock from small workshops and individual journeymen. The really fashionable retail establishments, however, maintained a direct connection with the actual making of furniture, and the whole activity, manufacture and retailing, took place under one roof. A German visitor, Sophie von La Roche, has left an account of her visit to Seddon's furniture-factory in Aldersgate, London, in 1786. She tells us that some 400 people were employed there – cabinet-makers, upholsterers, carvers, gilders, mirror-makers and (unusually for England) ormolu workers. The various trades represented within a large manufactory such as Seddon's nevertheless retained a certain independence, reflected in the fact that each workman was expected to supply his own chest of tools which remained personal property, as is still the case in certain sections of the furniture trade today. When Seddon's was destroyed in a blaze, the loss of the chests of tools was considered the most serious consequence of the disaster.

Both England and France exported a good deal of furniture, but the exports seem on the whole to have been of different kinds. Despite the rise of neo-classicism, the French retained a reputation for fashion and luxury. At the very end of the century the neo-classical architect Henry Holland and his Whig clients were still enamoured of certain aspects of French taste, and George Hepplewhite's pattern-book contained some extremely 'correct' French designs. Both the *ébéniste*

97, 98 Weisweiler and the great French chair-maker Georges Jacob supplied furniture for the Prince of Wales's splendid new mansion Carlton House, on the site of what is now Carlton House Terrace. At the Revolution, the English were also not ashamed to buy the best French furniture second hand, including much that had previously adorned Versailles and other royal palaces. A great deal remains to this day in English collections, and there are particularly splendid examples in the collection of H.M. the Queen, inherited from George IV.

English trade was on the whole more mundane, and was based on the very high reputation enjoyed by the English furniture-industry for practicality of design as well as quality of craftsmanship. In the eighteenth century Russia, Denmark, Germany, Holland, Flanders, Poland, Spain and Portugal are all known to have been regular importers of furniture of English make. In the first half of the century, the period for which the customs returns give detailed information, the types of furniture exported included cabinets, chairs, chests-of-drawers, secretaires, clockcases, looking-glasses, picture-frames

97 Weisweiler side-table
supplied to George IV, when
Prince of Wales, for Carlton
House

98 Louis XVI *fauteuil à la turque*
by Jacob

and upholstery – in fact, almost every conceivable commodity in this line. Furniture was often specially designed to please the overseas customer. For example, lacquer furniture in especially bright colours and rush-seated chairs went to Spain, where there was particular enthusiasm for English workmanship. One fine set of red lacquer furniture, made by the leading London cabinet-maker Giles Grendey, remained in the possession of the Spanish Duques de Infantado until 1935.

99

One very important part of the English export trade was to England's American colonies, but here a distinction must be made. Much English furniture went to the rich southern colonies, in return for agricultural products and other raw materials. The northern colonies were already developing in a different way, with their own manufactures, and had less to offer the mother country. As a result, it was here that an independent American furniture-industry first developed, basing itself on English prototypes, but also evolving certain recognizably local forms, such as the block-front bureau. The best of these pieces were equal to anything made in England at the same time – in fact, America was the only region outside the British Isles where British furniture-makers had to compete with craftsmen

100

99 Red lacquer day-bed by Grendey

100 Eighteenth-century American mahogany block-front bureau

of their own race and with a similar level of skill. This also tended to restrict the market for furniture shipped across the Atlantic.

In addition to exporting actual furniture, England also exported skill. A number of foreign craftsmen came to complete their training in England, and it was a mark of distinction to have done so. Abraham Roentgen, founder of the great German furniture-making concern at *86* Neuwied, trained in London; so too did Georg Haupt, the leading Swedish furniture-maker of the late eighteenth century. Roentgen's son David, who brought his father's business to new heights of success, styled himself *Englischer Kabinettmacher*, so great was the prestige of English workmanship.

101 David, *The Loves of Paris and Helen* (Salon of 1789).
The furniture resembles that designed by the painter for his own studio

102 American neo-classical decoration. Study by Alexander Jackson Davis for
a Greek Revival double parlour, *c.* 1830

CHAPTER SEVEN

1800–1850

In many respects furniture changed more fundamentally in the first half of the nineteenth century than it had during the preceding 200 years. The changes were technological as well as stylistic. The only comparable epoch is the period from 1945 until the present.

The technological revolution, however, gathered pace only slowly. At first it was style that counted. It was discussed as never before. Neo-classicism may have combined purely fashionable with new intellectual and moral elements, but it did not bring with it great changes in actual processes of manufacture. This conservatism was at least partly due to the fact that, like all previous movements of style, it developed hierarchically. That is to say, the style-setters continued to be those who were at the top of the social heap. Radical designers and architects still worked for moneyed and aristocratic patrons.

The sources of neo-classicism, as well as the whole process of diffusion, were markedly different in England and in France. In England, Adam, and after him Holland, represent the first phase. The next, and much stricter one is represented by Thomas Hope. Neo-classicism, like Palladianism, was therefore the product of an alliance between architects, connoisseurs and patrons. In France, however, it was established as an official style.   *103, 104*

Unlike Adam and Holland, Hope was not a professional architect, but a dilettante and a man of means, concerned first and foremost with creating a sympathetic environment for himself and his collections; and after that with diffusing ideas about the decorative arts which for him at least took on a moral overtone. This tendency to draw moral lessons from the inanimate objects with which people surrounded themselves was to be extremely characteristic of the whole of the nineteenth century; it appears powerfully both in the second phase of the Gothic revival, and afterwards in the Arts and Crafts Movement.

Hope belonged to a well-known Dutch banking family. He was born in 1768, and from 1786 onwards spent a number of years travelling in Europe and the Middle East, in pursuit of classical remains. In 1795 the French invasion of Holland drove his family out, and Hope thereafter made his base in England. In 1801, he bought the surviving part of Sir William Hamilton's collection of Greek vases (the rest had gone down with the *Colossus* off the Scillies). His thought was to create appropriate settings for these treasures, for his Italian and Dutch paintings, and for the contemporary neo-classical sculptures which he also collected. He had two homes: a house in Duchess Street, London, which he bought in 1799, and which had already been completely remodelled by 1804 (significantly enough the decorations Hope destroyed were by Adam); and a country mansion called The Deepdene in Surrey. In 1807 he published a book called *Household Furniture and Interior Decoration from Designs by Thomas Hope*. This illustrates the interiors of the London house. The house itself was demolished in 1851, but much of the furniture survived at The Deepdene, to be dispersed at auction in 1917. Surviving pieces can still be identified from the plates in Hope's book.

104

Hope wanted to endow his furniture with three qualities: character, beauty, and what he called 'appropriate meaning'. Much of it was intended to be symbolic; not all of it was by any standard comfortable. But it did put the case for the new purified 'Greek' taste

103 'Egyptian' chair designed by Hope, *c.* 1805

104 The 'Egyptian' Room in Hope's London house. From his *Household Furniture and Interior Decoration*, 1807

which Hope supported. This taste was based on a clearer understanding of the difference between Greek and Roman styles, brought about by books like James Stuart and N. Revett's *Antiquities of Athens*, which made genuine Greek buildings at last available to the European public. Greek taste was consciously chastened and simple. Adam, who had based himself on studies in Italy and at Spalato, now looked fussy and over-elaborate to the connoisseurs of Hope's generation. In some respects, however, Hope remained quite firmly conservative. His house was intended as a show-place, and the rooms were arranged with the formality of a museum.

Despite this, his ideas were extremely influential; and they were popularized and made more practical in a cabinet-maker's pattern-book which appeared in 1808, the year after the publication of *Household Furniture*. George Smith's *A Collection of Designs for Household Furniture and Interior Decoration* is as much the authority for the classical version of the Regency style as Chippendale's *Director* is   105

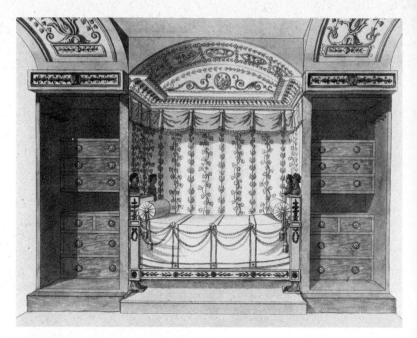

105 Smith, French bed and wardrobe. From *A Collection of Designs for Household Furniture and Interior Decoration*, 1808

for the varieties of English rococo. Smith's furniture, like Hope's, is robust. It can also be ornate, and even coarse. But it is furniture and decoration for the well-to-do home rather than the palace, and this is one of the things which distinguishes English furniture of the period from what was being made at the same time in France.

Unlike its English equivalent, French early nineteenth-century furniture shows the effect of a change of patronage rather than of a sharp break in style. There was, in fact, and despite the upheaval caused by the French Revolution, a direct continuity of development from late Louis XVI, through the period of the Directoire and Consulate, to the furniture of the Empire and even to that of the Restauration. Standard forms – those of armchairs or chests-of-drawers, for example – were continuously modified to cater for changes in taste, but the beginning and end of the sequence of development still show a recognizable relationship. The changes which took place were strongly influenced by one man: Napoleon I.

120

106 *Lit éxécuté à Paris pour M? O.* Design by Percier and Fontaine

107 *The Music Room at Malmaison.* Watercolour by Auguste Garneray, *c.* 1800

Napoleon's self-identification with the emperors who ruled Rome, and his desire to create a recognizable image for his own regime, glorifying its military successes, bred in him a strong distaste for the idea of reusing the furniture, however splendid, which had been left behind by his Bourbon predecessors. He therefore initiated a programme for refurnishing and redecorating the various royal palaces, particularly the Tuileries and Fontainebleau. Another *107* important Napoleonic residence was Malmaison, which bore the stamp of the Empress Josephine's taste rather than Napoleon's, and was decorated in a feminine version of the new manner. The chief *106* creators of the Empire style were the designers Charles Percier and Pierre-François-Léonard Fontaine, whose *Recueil des décorations intérieures* was published in 1801 and reissued in 1812.

The engravings in this collection did much to popularize the style, and so, too, did well-attended exhibitions of the 'products of French industry'; one was held in 1802 in the courtyard of the Louvre, and one in 1806 on the Esplanade des Invalides.

On a more personal level, the leading painters of the time continued to have a hand in creating Empire taste, just as they had done in the last years of the Ancien Régime. Jacques Louis David *101* designed furniture for his own studio; Pierre Paul Prud'hon designed a dressing-table for Napoleon's second wife, Marie-Louise of Austria, and a cradle for her son the King of Rome.

The furniture that resulted from all these efforts had great unity. It was provided with a consistent grammar of ornament and often took the form of classical architecture translated into different terms. The ebonized columns, gilt capitals and other ornaments, and flamboyant mahogany veneers typical of the style gave it an assertiveness suitable to a parvenu regime. This assertiveness, in addition to its logic and coherence, made it influential throughout Europe, and also in America. In countries outside France, it often arrived in the wake of Napoleonic conquests. The most striking example of this is in Italy, where the small kingdoms Napoleon founded for the benefit of his relations were centres of diffusion. Some of the most elegant Italian Empire furniture was created in Florence, where Napoleon's sister Elisa Baciocchi ruled as Grand Duchess of Tuscany. But the great centre of production was Naples, ruled first by the Emperor's brother Joseph and then by his sister Caroline and her husband Marshal Murat. In fact, the Empire style became so firmly rooted in

108 Mahogany side-chair made
by Phyfe, 1807

the Italian consciousness as suitable furnishing for palaces that it persisted long after Napoleon's fall.

In Russia, the Emperor Alexander's admiration for Napoleon led to a widespread adoption of Empire motifs. A particularly notable instance of Russian Empire furnishing and decoration is the work done by Andrei Voronikhin at the palace of Pavlovsk.

In the United States there was a mingling of English Regency and French Empire influences. A very elegant original version of the Regency style was evolved by the New York cabinet-maker Duncan Phyfe. But he met with competition from French cabinet-makers *108* who emigrated to America after the Revolution. One of these imigrants was Honoré Lannuier, who arrived in New York in 1803. His furniture often has metal mounts in the French manner, and is generally more elaborate than Phyfe's work. The Greek revival style long persisted in American furniture, just as it did in American *102* architecture.

Perhaps the most interesting offshoot of the Empire style was the creation of Biedermeier furniture in the Austrian dominions and *109* some parts of Germany. The word Biedermeier implies bourgeois comfort, and the style originated only after the Empire itself had passed from the scene. It was fed by three springs: Empire taste, Louis XVI and English Regency. Though the forms often seem at first sight to be borrowed from Empire originals, in a deeper sense the furniture itself represents a reaction against French taste and French ambitions. The woods used were usually native fruitwoods; furniture ceased to be architecture in miniature and became a direct expression of the processes used to produce it. One modern authority says: 'Neither before nor in the period of historicism which followed was a style's development from its raw material as important a factor as it was during the Biedermeier period.'

The pieces categorized as Biedermeier can either be very simple or very elaborate. Some, such as the workboxes in the shape of globes, seem designed to push the carpenter's skill to the very limits. Others, notably the big secretaires, have a massive, monumental quality which is reminiscent of the cupboards and chests produced in Germany during the sixteenth century. But basically the emphasis was on simplicity, practicality, comfort and lack of ostentation. In many respects Biedermeier is the true forerunner of the functional furniture produced during the present century, which emerged in the first place from the same Central European milieu.

111

Even French Empire furniture, though stiffer and more pompous than Biedermeier, has within it a strongly rational element. Speaking of chairs, for example, Percier and Fontaine observe that 'of all the possible shapes for a seat there are some which are dictated by the shape of the human body and by questions of sheer necessity and convenience, so that instinct alone would lead one to them'. Empire designers were occasionally prepared to accommodate the particular needs of the time. One example is the so-called *chaise à l'officier*, an armchair with the arms missing but with the front supports for them still present. The idea was that such a chair could accommodate a man in uniform still wearing his sabre. Chairs of this type conjure up a vivid picture of the military comings and goings in the fashionable houses occupied by members of Napoleon's court.

110

In France itself, the one major concession to fantasy lay in the use of Egyptian motifs. These were inspired by Napoleon's campaign in Egypt in 1798, and in particular by the engravings of Baron Vivant Denon, who accompanied him there. The Egyptian style was later to

109 Biedermeier furniture. Austrian walnut chair, c. 1820–25

110 *Chaise à l'officier*, mahogany and ormolu. By Giovanni Socchi, Florence, c. 1810

111 Mechanical desk by Socchi, Florence, c. 1810

112 Couch in the form of an Egyptian boat with crocodile feet. English, 1806–10

103, 104 be taken up in England, where it was made fashionable by Nelson's victory in the Battle of the Nile. English furniture using Egyptian details shows far less restraint than the French equivalent, and some really extraordinary objects were produced, such as a couch with 112 crocodile feet. These, like the chinoiserie and commemorative furniture produced in England at the same epoch, have no real parallel in France.

Regency chinoiserie is, of course, best exemplified by the 93 furnishings of the Prince Regent's own Royal Pavilion, and these have for the most part been reassembled, and can be seen in their original setting. One consequence of the fashion for chinoiserie at the beginning of the nineteenth century was the popularity of pieces either made of bamboo or of beechwood carved and painted to resemble bamboo. This was a fashion which was to appear in a new form in the Aesthetic 1880s.

Commemorative furniture, like furniture in the Egyptian style, was chiefly connected with the cult of Nelson and his victories. The most widespread example of the commemorative impulse is the so-called Trafalgar chair, with part of the back carved to resemble twisted rope. Far more extravagant is the superb Trafalgar Suite, now 113 at the Royal Pavilion in Brighton, where everything possible is supported by gilded dolphins. Furniture of this kind already foreshadows the early Victorian taste for the opulent and the complex, and has more than a hint of typically Victorian eclecticism.

The apparent confusion of styles visible in English and to some extent in Continental and American furniture after the year 1830 or thereabouts has caused people to speak of a radical degeneration of both taste and technique, and also of an inability on the part of furniture-designers to invent forms that were both suitable to their purpose and expressive of a coherent stylistic attitude, an ability which was only partially recovered after the reform initiated by the Arts and Crafts Movement later in the century. The bulk of recent research into what is, in fact, an extremely complicated period of furniture history has concentrated on what took place in England; moreover, English developments appear to encompass nearly everything which is to be found elsewhere (for example, the world-wide fashion for the Gothic which had its roots in English soil); and so I shall for the moment concentrate on England.

113 The Trafalgar Suite. Made by William Collins and presented to Greenwich Hospital in 1813 in memory of Nelson

114 Early nineteenth-century Gothic. The drawing-room at Eaton Hall, Cheshire, 1826

A young English couple aiming to furnish a fairly substantial house in, say, the year 1835, would have been faced with an embarrassment of choice. The furniture available to them included a heavier version of Hope's Greek style, sometimes also called the Modern; a new version of Gothic; a version of Tudor; and another of Louis XIV. There was also a kind of non-style which has subsequently been dubbed Naturalistic. A version of renaissance style was to become current during the 1840s. Collecting antique furniture was already a hobby with a few; and in addition there was a substantial business in making up new furniture from bits of old carving. Much furniture in the so-called Tudor style was produced like this.

As it happens, our imaginary couple would probably not have settled for one style throughout the house. Certain styles were considered more suitable for men, and others for women. A 'masculine' room, such as the dining-room, would be done up in

Greek or Gothic – the Greek was much favoured for men's clubs – while a 'feminine' room, such as the drawing-room, would be furnished in a version of rococo.

The Greek style, since it is simply a heavier derivation of familiar Regency patterns, need not take up much space here. The Gothic and the Tudor are more interesting. Gothic of one sort or another had of course persisted in furniture since the mid eighteenth century, and Gothic details are often found even on quite plain Regency pieces; thus, for example, a Gothic touch would be given to the glazing-bars of bookcases. Smith's *Household Furniture* of 1808, in addition to designs based on Hope, offers a full range of Gothic patterns, and furniture of this type soon became established as something especially suitable for libraries. The great propagandist for a more serious approach to the Gothic made his appearance in the late 1820s. This was Augustus Welby Northmore Pugin, born in 1812, who at the age of fifteen was already designing Gothic furniture for Windsor Castle. *115*

Pugin's attitude towards the Gothic changed when he was converted to Catholicism in 1835. For him it became what neo-classicism had been to Thomas Hope. Gothic was now no longer a style but a crusade against what was frivolous and immoral, a kind of religion in itself. Adapting Gothic forms empirically to suit

115 Mid nineteenth-century Gothic. Chair made for Scarisbrick Hall and designed by Pugin, *c.* 1840

contemporary needs was no longer enough – it was necessary to evolve a complete grammar of Gothic construction and ornament. Pugin's study of medieval joinery led him more and more to emphasize rational structure, and to make an open display of constructional features quite foreign to the cabinet-making practice of the day. In 1835 he published *Gothic Furniture of the Fifteenth Century*, an immensely influential collection of designs. From 1836 onwards he worked with the architect Charles Barry on the interiors of the new Houses of Parliament, and these are still the best surviving examples of early Victorian Gothic. But, while Pugin's Gothic, with its moral fervour, long retained its position as a style for church-furnishing and for certain kinds of public commission, most people thought it a trifle harsh for ordinary domestic use.

More favoured was the closely related Elizabethan taste. This received a huge impetus from the contemporary fashion for the novels of Walter Scott. At its best, this has almost the coherence of the Gothic itself. The architect Anthony Salvin, for example, designed fine country-house interiors at Mamhead in Devon and at Scotney
116 Castle in Kent, dating from the late 1820s to the early 1840s. But it was more difficult to compose a satisfactory set of rules to guide the designer, and much Victorian 'Elizabethan' furniture is a strange mixture which relies as much on late Stuart forms as it does on those of the furniture made a century earlier.

The Louis XIV taste was even more of a jumble. It was inspired by a renewal of influence from France (just as the French took up the English Gothic revival and turned it into the far more frivolous *style troubadour*). A lack of knowledge about what Louis XIV furniture had really looked like led to ideas and shapes being borrowed freely from a wide range of baroque and rococo sources, so that much Victorian Louis XIV is actually much closer to full-blown Louis XV.

Both Louis XIV and Gothic made their contribution to the
117 Naturalistic style. From the various versions of Louis came the preference for swelling curves and an over-all rotundity, especially in upholstered furniture; from Gothic came the liking for ornament derived directly from nature, as illustrated in Pugin's *Floriated Ornament* (1849). This was based on a botanical book of 1590 identifying the plants from which certain Gothic ornaments were taken.

The development of Naturalistic furniture had more than stylistic significance. It reflected a new yearning for comfort, and it was this,

116 'Elizabethan' taste. The library at Scotney Castle as redesigned by Salvin, late 1820s–early 1840s

more than anything else, that was responsible for novelty of form rather than ornament. Even at the century's beginning the desire for a more comfortable way of life was beginning to grow. In part, this desire was the product of deprivation. People at that period had to struggle both with the consequences of a long war and with those of a steadily increasing population. Among the more prosperous it was said that the war 'doubled the cost and trebled the difficulty of genteel living'. This encouraged many of them to concentrate on what was practical rather than on what was showy, and much good-quality Regency furniture is therefore distinguished by a sober fitness for use. A little lower down the social scale, members of the middle and lower middle class were forced to live in increasingly cramped conditions, especially in towns. The housing-stock had not increased commensurately with greater numbers. There was therefore an urgent need for portable, adaptable and space-saving furniture, and designers were encouraged to continue the experiments made in this sphere during the eighteenth century, but now concentrating more than

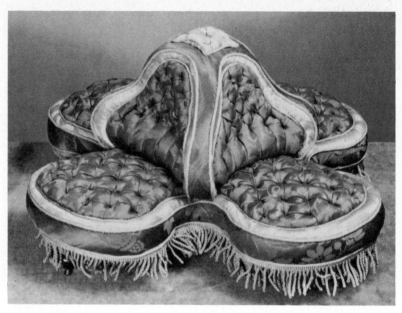

117 Naturalistic furniture. Early Victorian button-upholstered circular sofa

ever before on fitness for use rather than luxury and novelty. Yet gradually, despite this loss of living space, there was a more general diffusion of furniture among the whole population, as a result of a general process of social and economic levelling. This, too, tended to put the emphasis on comfort and practicality, rather than show.

From the 1830s onwards the situation eased, and mere·compactness ceased to be of such primary importance. People's minds nevertheless remained fixed on the idea of an easier, and also a more informal way of living. The change was apparent in the arrangement of furniture even before it affected actual design. In 1807 Lady Wharncliffe thought, when visiting Hornby Castle in Yorkshire, that it 'would be perfectly comfortable but that there is nothing in it but the old furniture, so that the rooms look *bare*'. In 1810 a French visitor to Osterley found the tables, sofas and chairs 'studiously *dérangés* about the fireplaces and in the middle of the rooms', even though the family were not living there and had not been in residence for some time: 'So much is the modern fashion of placing furniture carried to an extreme, as fashions always are, that the apartments of a fashionable house look like an upholsterer's or cabinet-maker's shop'. This description is confirmed by an often-quoted passage in Jane Austen's *Persuasion* (written in 1815–16, published in 1818). The old-fashioned square parlour of a great mansion has been given 'the proper air of confusion by a grand piano forte and a harp, flower-stands and little tables placed in every direction'.

The characteristic rotundity of Naturalistic seat-furniture, and its *117* unaccustomed degree of comfort, were both due to an important innovation – the introduction of sprung upholstery. The honour of inventing this seems to belong to an Austrian. One Georg Junigl, a Viennese upholsterer, received a patent in 1822 for his improvement on contemporary methods of furniture upholstery. This mentions 'the assistance of iron springs'. The first English patent for sprung upholstery was taken out by Samuel Pratt, Camp Equipage Maker of New Bond Street, on 24 December 1828. This was for 'wire springs in beds, cushions, etc.'. Nevertheless, the innovation gained ground rather slowly, and in some circles deep-sprung upholstery was still thought of as a luxurious novelty as late as the 1850s.

Sprung upholstery was part of a general search for new materials and new processes taking place at this time. One important innovation was the changeover from wooden to metal beds which *118*

118 Brass four-poster bed in renaissance style, made by R. W. Winfield, 1851

began in the 1840s. The reasons were largely hygienic. Bed-bugs were a constant nuisance, and the old wooden beds of the eighteenth century had to be completely dismantled at least once a year if there was to be any hope of keeping the creatures in check. The metal bed, which discouraged them almost completely, became a great and continuing success. By the mid 1850s these beds had become an important branch of manufacture in England, and by 1875 some 6,000 were being produced every week, half of them for export. Metal was also used, though more desultorily, for making chairs. Some were rather crude, like the two chairs with tubular metal legs, cast-irons backs and wooden seats designed by Robert Mallet (later the designer of the Fastnet Rock lighthouse) and published in Loudon's *Encylopaedia of Cottage, Farm and Villa Architecture and Furniture*, which appeared in 1833. Others were extremely elegant, such as the rocking-chair made of brass tube exhibited at the Great Exhibition of 1851, which anticipates the Bauhaus. There was also another pattern of rocking-chair equally elegant, made of strip steel with upholstery. This suits twentieth-century interiors so well that copies were produced commercially in the 1960s. On the whole, however, the Victorians preferred to obscure technical innovation with a plethora of ornament, so such functional designs are few. But

119

119 Victorian metal rocking chair, *c*. 1850

120 Mid nineteenth-century papier-mâché settee with mother-of-pearl decoration

ornament could be used well, as in some of the charming cast-iron furniture in 'rustic' designs which was produced at this time, mostly for use outdoors.

One especially popular material in the period 1835–70 was papier- *120* mâché. This was not new – it had been known in the eighteenth century – but the Victorians used it in novel ways, and on a much bigger scale than heretofore. The best quality was made by pressing wetted spongy paper into a mould; a less good quality by using actual paper pulp which could be formed under pressure. Papier-mâché had many advantages: it was cheap, it made an excellent ground for japanned decoration, and it was easy to create elaborate simulated inlay in mother-of-pearl. This was done by first applying a thin layer of mother-of-pearl to the whole surface, then painting the design in varnish, then finally removing areas not protected by the varnish by means of acid. The material was used chiefly for small articles, such as boxes and trays, and for light pieces of furniture – small cane-seated chairs, firescreens, little tables and so forth. Occasionally more ambitious articles were attempted, but these would usually have metal or wooden frameworks to support the colourful papier-mâché panels.

The most truly radical of all the furniture-making innovations of the period was pioneered, like sprung upholstery, in Austria. The man responsible was Michael Thonet. Thonet grew up as a craftsman in the Biedermeier ambiance, with its emphasis on simplicity and practicality. From about the year 1830, he began to experiment with new techniques for making furniture without the usual carving and jointing of the wood. The solution he first hit on was partly derived from shipbuilding, and consisted in using heat and water to bend thin strips of wood, which were laminated together and forced into the shape desired. By 1841 Thonet was sufficiently far advanced with his experiments to take out patents in France, England and Belgium; and in the 1840s he used his new methods to make furniture which was supplied to the Liechtenstein palace in Vienna. The models Thonet devised in order to fulfil this prestigious commission were the forerunners of the bentwood furniture, now made of solid wood steamed and bent into shape, which captured a great slice of the European and American mass-market in the second half of the century; and which continues to be produced today, using much the same techniques. Thonet furniture has a dateless elegance which springs from the perfect mating of the desired form and the particular method of manufacture.

Another furniture-manufacturer who began to make use of lamination in the 1840s was the American, John Henry Belter, though his attitude towards his material was less questing and radical than Thonet's. Belter made furniture in the nineteenth-century rococo taste; indeed, his was a more elegant version of it than the one that evolved in Europe. His flowing forms were emphasized by delicate naturalistic carving, pierced in many places. This could only be safely achieved by the use of laminated panels; layers of wood, each only a sixteenth of an inch thick, were glued together so that the grain of one layer always ran in the opposite direction from that of the next. Between six and eight layers of wood were used, and the panels thus formed were steamed and bent into shape in moulds before being carved.

Despite these innovations, the furniture-industry everywhere tended to remain one of the more conservative areas of manufacture. It has sometimes been said that the Industrial Revolution profoundly affected furniture and the way it was made, that a kind of holocaust of craftsmanship took place. This is very far from being true. Furniture-

136

121 Thonet bentwood single chair, 1850s

122 Side-chair in laminated rosewood by Belter. American, 1840–60

making had long been a piece-work industry, where each job passed through a number of hands before it was completed. But in England, then the most highly industrialized of all nations, there were no signs, in the period 1800–50, of the establishment of a factory system in anything like the modern sense. Indeed the complete production of furniture by mechanical means was not a nineteenth-century phenomenon at all, and has even been relatively slow to establish itself in our own day. Machines, despite the fact that a whole series of patents were taken out, were accepted only reluctantly. As late as 1874 a writer in the *Furniture Trade Gazette* noted that the use of woodworking machinery was still being questioned as uneconomic. Some mechanical aids found a warmer welcome than others. By 1829

137

steam-driven machines for cutting veneers were already in use. These greatly diminished cost and extended the market for veneered furniture, thus to some extent bringing it into disrepute. 'Veneering', as a term of social contempt, was already in use by the beginning of Victoria's reign: the image does not originate with Charles Dickens. Another way in which the machine had an impact was in the use of a rotary cutter for speedy chamfering. In general, it became easier to produce all ornamental carved details. Those in charge of furniture-workshops must have been grateful that this kind of help was available to them, as neo-classicism's distaste for almost all forms of carved ornament had indeed led to huge and irrecoverable losses of traditional skill in this particular branch of work. In the early nineteenth century there were only eleven master carvers and about sixty journeymen carvers still at work in the whole of London.

During the first third of the century, craft standards in general remained very high. The French furniture of the Restauration period, for instance, was often much better finished in certain details than that produced under the Ancien Régime. Carcasses for chests-of-drawers were made of better wood and the drawers ran more smoothly. The best-quality Biedermeier furniture was equally admirable in workmanship, and so was that produced by the English cabinet-maker George Bullock. Bullock, like his Biedermeier contempo-raries, experimented with native timbers, in his case larch and bog oak. If, towards the year 1850, hand craftsmanship showed signs of a decline, this was due not so much to actual industrialization as to the pressure to produce a great quantity of work, often in sweated labour conditions, and to the intensification of the piece-work system. As soon as the decline became painfully noticeable, voices such as those of John Ruskin and William Morris were raised to condemn it.

In the first half of the nineteenth century the most impressive feature is not the restless proliferation of styles, nor indeed the energetic impulse towards ornament and yet more ornament. It is the repetition of a process which had already been in operation during the seventeenth century, but now on a wider scale and in a more decisive way. There was a steady emergence of what one can only call furniture archetypes. Sometimes these are born through the energy and persistence of one man; this is the case, for instance, with the furniture designed by Thonet. But often it happens because a certain furniture-type establishes its fitness for a particular task to the point

123 English cabinet in the manner of Bullock, early nineteenth century

where no one thinks of changing it much. Chairs are especially apt to win this kind of acceptance. One example is the light Italian *chiavari* chair, which was originally a neo-classical invention (an example which belonged to Queen Hortense Bonaparte closely resembles those which are still made today). Other and even more striking instances are to be found in the development of the Windsor chair in both England and America; and in the Shaker-manufactured ladder- back and rocker. The stick-back Windsor chair perhaps achieved its ultimate perfection of form in the hands of early nineteenth-century American craftsmen, while at the same time sustaining the fortunes of

125
124

139

124 Maplewood Shaker side-chair, mid nineteenth century

the High Wycombe furniture-workshops in England. Shaker furniture, with its magnificent simplicity, is closely akin in spirit to the best American Windsor chairs, though mostly somewhat later in date; Shaker furniture only acquires a recognizable identity after about 1815. Its uniformity of style reflects the gospel conviction of the religious communities from which it came. They felt that 'nothing short of union in all things [could] constitute a true church'. The Shakers found a ready market for what they made because it was clearly superior to anything else of the same sort which happened to be available. It was they who seem to have popularized the rocking-chair in the United States, a detail of social custom which was noted by all European visitors. In 1838, for example, an English builder called James Frewin recorded: 'In America it is considered a compliment to give the stranger the rocking-chair as a seat; and when there is more than one kind in the house, the stranger is always presented with the best.'

One particular sort of 'classic' early nineteenth-century furniture was the kind provided for travellers. This had its origins in the camp furniture of the Napoleonic Wars, and demand was stimulated by the increase in overseas travel after 1815. Cabin space was often let empty for a long voyage, and people took their own furniture with them, especially if they were emigrating for good. What they took was compact, practical and simple, and with hindsight we can see in it the beginnings of our own functional tradition.

Furniture of this kind is in the sharpest possible contrast to the exuberant show-pieces which attracted attention at the Great Exhibition of 1851, and at first it seems incredible that two such different approaches to the same needs should have coexisted. Yet both reflect essential aspects of the time. Exhibition furniture is the statement the Victorians made about themselves. As Edward T. Joy remarks in his recent excellent study *English Furniture, 1800–1851*, it 'reflected completely the assertion of opulence and faith in mechanical progress which, coupled with nostalgia for the past, made up the temper of 1851'. Simple travelling furniture, on the other hand, was the direct and practical response to the physical dynamism of the age, which was rapidly taking the furniture-designer and everyone else outside the boundaries which had been set for them almost since the beginning of recorded history.

125 American
Windsor settee, *c.* 1800

126 'Thirteenth-century' headboard designed by Burges, with inset
painting by Henry Holiday

CHAPTER EIGHT

1850–1914

Furniture in the second half of the nineteenth century was not as innovative from the technical point of view as it had been during the first half. In some ways, there was a conscious rebellion against innovations of this sort, and an accompanying desire to return to a partly imaginary 'honesty' and 'simplicity' of construction. On the other hand, this period was extremely prolific when it came to the invention of new forms.

Some of the styles which had been popular during the first half of the century began to die out. One was the Gothic; after 1850, there was a shift from Pugin's fourteenth-century Gothic to the supposedly purer forms of the thirteenth century which were the passion, for example, of the architect and furniture-designer William Burges.   *126*
But, since there was very little surviving concrete evidence for them, designers were forced back upon their own invention. Some of the solutions they came up with were so outlandish and impractical that after about 1870 the Gothic as a whole began to lose popularity.

One style that did continue was the neo-classical, which had flourished in one form or another since before 1800. But this now started to undergo an interesting transformation, which affected furniture in England, in France and in the United States. This was the return to late eighteenth-century styles, and in particular to the Louis XVI. In the United States, for example, the Louis XVI revival which appeared in the late 1860s and early 1870s was usually dubbed the 'neo-grec'. Sometimes it was combined with influences borrowed from the renaissance. In France, there was a particular reason why Louis XVI should suddenly become ultra-fashionable, and this was the Empress Eugénie's cult of Marie-Antoinette. This led to the evolution of a mode of decoration which is sometimes called 'Louis Seize Impératrice', and which was seen in its most concentrated guise   *128*
in the palace of Compiègne and in other imperial residences. However, other grand French interiors of the same period, such as those in the two mansions of Princesse Mathilde, recorded for us in a   *127*

143

series of detailed watercolours done between 1854 and 1864, are more eclectic, and show little trace of commitment to one furnishing style in particular.

In both England and France there was now much greater knowledge of and interest in antique furniture. This led both to the production of extremely skilful copies and to the recarving and sometimes repainting of old pieces to make them seem richer and more elaborate. In Paris the best copyists made facsimiles of some of the most famous pieces produced for the Bourbon kings, with a particular penchant for imitating late Louis XVI cabinet-makers such as Weisweiler. In England, very skilful imitations were made of the classic eighteenth-century styles: Chippendale, Hepplewhite and Thomas Sheraton. Some of these copies subsequently entered museums, and one or two (in the Victoria and Albert Museum, for example) were detected as such only recently, and then only by the examination of concealed details such as the interior upholstery of seat-furniture. Other fakes or copies probably still remain undetected, even in the great national collections. They provide a striking proof that not all Victorian cabinet-makers had lost their skill, nor indeed their taste and sense of proportion.

At a somewhat lower level, the multiplication of grand hotels, which were among the most typical products of the Victorian railway age, led to a demand for furniture in period styles to match the interiors. The so-called 'Louis' styles came to be considered more and more as the only suitable ones for hotel use, and this led to the birth of a simplified and commercialized Louis XVI which later acquired the flippant nickname 'Louis the hotel'.

A more personal variant of the eighteenth century was created by some artists. Contemporary watercolours show what appears to be Sheraton furniture in Dante Gabriel Rossetti's Cheyne Walk studio; but a closer examination of the surviving pieces associated with him suggests that they were in fact designed in eighteenth-century idiom by the artist himself.

The Pre-Raphaelite Movement to which Rossetti belonged is, however, more often connected with something very different: the strong revulsion against commercial Victorian design which led to the birth of the Arts and Crafts Movement. The story of this is considerably more complicated than it appears at first, and it is possible to distinguish at least three different phases of development.

129

127 Nineteenth-century eclectic. Princesse Mathilde's library at Saint-Gratien. Watercolour by Charles Giraud

The first is connected with Ruskin and Morris; the second with the so-called Aesthetic Movement; and the third was the fully developed Arts and Crafts. All three phases are represented in England, and the second and third also had a powerful impact in the United States.

Ruskin was not a designer, but a theorist and moralist, and one of his passions was for honesty of expression, material and workmanship, qualities which he thought the architecture of his time conspicuously lacked. One of the things he most detested was the division of labour: 'It is not, truly speaking, the labour that is divided, but the men: – divided into mere segments of men – broken into small fragments and crumbs of life; so that all the little piece of intelligence that is left in a man is not enough to make a pin, or a nail, but exhausts itself in making the point of a pin or the head of a nail.' Ruskin thought that a just society must obey what he called 'three broad and simple rules':

'1. Never encourage the manufacture of any article not strictly necessary, in the production of which *Invention* has no share.

128 'Louis Seize Impératrice'. The Cabinet de Travail at the Château de Compiègne. Watercolour by J. B. Fortune de Fournier

'2. Never demand exact finish for its own sake, but only for some practical or noble end.

'3. Never encourage copying or imitation of any kind, except for the sake of preserving records of great works.'

In pursuance of his ideals, Ruskin agreed, in 1854, to teach at the Working Men's College which had been founded in that same year by the Christian Socialist, F.D. Maurice. This brought him into personal touch with the members of the Pre-Raphaelite Brotherhood, a group of young artists whom he had already championed in print. Among the artists connected with the Working Men's College were Rossetti, Edward Burne-Jones, Ford Madox Brown and Arthur Hughes. The practical moving force in a new attitude to design was, however, to be none of these, but Burne-Jones's associate, Morris.

Morris and Burne-Jones had known each other since they arrived in Oxford as students in 1853. This was the year in which the second

131

146

129 Rossetti's sitting-room at Cheyne Walk, with Sheraton revival furniture designed by Rossetti. Watercolour by Treffy Dunn, 1882

and third volumes of Ruskin's *The Stones of Venice* were published, and Morris immediately read them, devoting special attention to the famous chapter entitled 'On the Nature of Gothic'. This chapter was the real credo of the Arts and Crafts Movement, and Ruskin had it reprinted as a separate pamphlet the next year, so that it could be distributed to the students of the Working Men's College.

The Pre-Raphaelites' interest in furniture sprang as much from their own personal needs as it did from Ruskin's plea for reform. They believed that art should be a totality; and they thought, too, that the applied arts should follow the same principles as their painting. Perhaps the first member of the circle to try his hand as a furniture-designer was Brown, who was never actually a member of the Brotherhood at all. The furniture he created derives rather obviously from Pugin, but is much plainer, simpler and more straightforward. Like Pugin's later furniture, it belonged to the tradition of joinery, rather than that of cabinet-making.

147

130 Morris & Co.'s first important commission: the Green Room by Webb for the South Kensington Museum, 1866

In 1860 Morris moved into the Red House designed for him by Philip Webb, and this increased his preoccupation with the decorative arts. The enterprise of the Red House led in turn to the foundation of Morris & Co., the Firm as Morris himself called it, the channel through which the new ideas about furniture and decoration were to be brought to the public. At the International Exhibition held at South Kensington in 1862 Morris & Co. scored a marked commercial success, and was, in addition, awarded two gold medals. At this point, Morris and his colleagues were still seen as medievalists, very much in the Pugin tradition. 'Messrs Morris & Company', read the jury's report, 'have exhibited several pieces of furniture, tapestries, etc., in the style of the Middle Ages. The general forms of the furniture, the arrangement of the tapestry, and the character of the details are satisfying to the archaeologist from the exactness of the imitation, and at the same time the general effect is excellent.'

130

148

The Firm prospered during the 1860s, and Morris himself became an outstandingly able designer of patterns for fabrics and wallpapers. Where furniture was concerned, the company's production fell into two categories, as Morris himself recognized. One kind he called 'necessary workaday furniture' which must, he thought, be kept 'simple to the last degree'; the other kind was 'state furniture'. Here there was no need to be sparing with ornament. On the contrary, 'we must', said Morris, 'make them as elegant and elaborate as we can with carving or inlaying or painting; these are the blossoms of the art of furniture'. Some of the simple designs devised by Morris & Co. were to enjoy a long and successful life. This was especially true of the variants they produced on the traditional Sussex rush-seated chair. *132* The elaborate pieces were less successful, probably because Morris himself was not so closely concerned with them.

Towards the end of the 1860s, furniture-design took a different turn from the one which Morris himself had seemed to indicate. The decisive date is probably 1868, which saw the publication of a book by Charles Lock Eastlake entitled *Hints on Household Taste*. The *133*

131 Stained wood chair with rush seat designed by Rossetti, and made by Morris & Co. in about 1865

132 Rush-seated chair designed by Madox Brown, *c.* 1860

133 Bookcase from Eastlake's *Hints on Household Taste*, 1868

134 (*opposite*) Satinwood cabinet with brass mountings, *c.* 1877, and ebonized oak chair, *c.* 1880, designed by Godwin

illustrations to this book did not seem to promise anything very radical; the text itself was a different matter. Eastlake preached a new kind of studied simplicity, and his teaching was, to the younger and more intelligent section of the Victorian middle class, a breath of fresh air. The book was very successful in England, and went on to be an even greater success in the United States, where it ran through a number of editions. Eastlake's name was, at least on the American side of the Atlantic, given to a certain kind of studiously plain and simple furniture. Throughout the 1870s interest in household decoration continued to increase, and in England there was a proliferation of magazines devoted to furniture towards the end of the decade. Significantly enough, these magazines devoted as much space to the amateur artist and craftsman as they did to the professional.

By this time the Aesthetic Movement – a new cult of the arts in general – had established itself, and so too had the concept of 'art furniture', as opposed to ordinary or commercial furniture. By the 1870s art furniture-manufacturers were being listed in the London Trade Directory in such a way as to make it plain that they fell into

quite a separate category from the ordinary cabinet-makers and furnishers. Art furniture was one of the more tangible symbols of the Aesthetic Movement, a general revolt on the part of younger members of the middle class against the accepted shibboleths of their day. One target of this revolt was moralizing in art, and in this sense the Aesthetic Movement and the furniture associated with it was a rejection of Ruskin and Morris. At the same time, there was a general impatience with whatever was familiar, a conscious search for the novel and the *outré*. The sources of art furniture were heterogeneous. There were still traces of Gothic influence. Furniture, though to a lesser degree than architecture, was also affected by the rise of the so-called Queen Anne style, something which Burges, speaking in 1875, attributed to the popularity of the historical novels of William Makepeace Thackeray. Finally, from the 1870s until the very end of the century, there was a strong current of influence from Japan. Art furniture discarded the heaviness, and also the comfort, of mid Victorian furniture in favour of a defiant spindliness. At first it was usually black, made of baywood, basswood, or black walnut. A little later, in the 1880s, there was a fashion for bright mahogany and satinwood. Furniture now had very thin, often turned legs. If carving was present, it was reduced to a design in incised gilt lines against an ebonized ground. Henry James got matters exactly right when, in his story *A New England Winter*, published in 1884, he referred to a character who was 'a votary of the newer school, and had made sacrifices to everything in black and gilt'.

In England, the architects Edward William Godwin and Charles Francis Annesley Voysey were among the most influential designers of furniture of this type; and Godwin, in particular, was extremely susceptible to Japanese influence. It was he who devised, not only new designs for furniture, but an entirely new kind of interior decoration, very sparse, with pale walls, painted rather than papered, and matting on the floor. Both Oscar Wilde and James McNeill Whistler had houses decorated in this manner.

It was Wilde who, on his celebrated lecture-tour of the United States in 1882–83, acted as the apostle of Aesthetic doctrines on the other side of the Atlantic. He was hugely successful, and the American home soon gave evidence of his impact. But even before Wilde's appearance on the scene, certain sophisticated American firms had been producing art furniture which paralleled what was being done in

England. Some of the best was made by Herter Brothers in New York. Christian Herter, who headed the firm, was born and trained in France, but his work, with its Japanese motifs, is in English rather than French taste. The offices of the architect Henry Hobson Richardson also produced what is recognizably art furniture, but this was in the second half of the 1880s.

The neo-Japanese style survived in America for a long period. Excellent and highly individual pieces of this type were still being produced in California during the first decade of the present century. They were designed by the architect Charles Sumner Greene for houses built by him in partnership with his younger brother, Henry Mather Greene.

The Aesthetic Movement did not, however, require its adherents to furnish their houses entirely anew. A mingling of antiques and Japanese decorative objects was an entirely acceptable formula, and the Aesthetic interior shades off into something that was merely 'artistic' in a general sense. The *mélange* of furniture and objects of different periods and of different types can be seen in representations of Rossetti's famous house in Cheyne Walk; and also in Atkinson Grimshaw's delightful painting of the interior of his own house. 129 136

Though the adherents of Aestheticism affected to despise commercialism, which they associated with everything philistine in their surroundings, most art furniture seems to have been commercially made. This is one of the things that separates it from the products of the Arts and Crafts Movement. Those connected with the latter wanted to change not merely the way furniture looked, but the whole process of making it. The Arts and Crafts Movement was a continuation and codification of the teachings of Ruskin and Morris. After a fallow period in the 1870s, Ruskinian idealism was revived with great vigour in the succeeding decade. The real beginning of the Movement can be dated to the year 1882, when the architect Arthur Heygate Mackmurdo founded the Century Guild. The avowed aim of this organization was to 'restore building, decoration, glass painting, pottery, wood-carving and metal to their rightful place beside painting and sculpture'. Mackmurdo's own furniture is not, however, very advanced in terms either of design or of construction. Much is still in the idiom pioneered by Morris, but there are a few examples which show a rather uneasy anticipation of fully-fledged Art Nouveau. 135

The Century Guild was followed in due course by the Art Workers' Guild, founded in 1884. The initial impetus here came from a discussion group founded by the pupils and assistants of the architect Richard Norman Shaw, one of the leading exponents of the Queen Anne style. But this organization deliberately shunned publicity, and it was not until the appearance of its offshoot, the Arts and Crafts Exhibition Society, that the new attitudes towards the crafts were given a public image.

Basically, following a lead already given by Pugin, the Arts and Crafts designers stood for a return to joiner-made furniture, and much of the technical progress made since the mid seventeenth century was deliberately discarded. This was done for two reasons. First in the name of honesty, which meant that no part of the construction must be concealed; second because the members of the Movement believed, like Ruskin, that piece-work was the enemy, that it was essential for every piece of furniture to be carried through from first to last by one man, since this must inevitably produce better work as well as greatly increased personal satisfaction. Like the furniture produced by Morris & Co., Arts and Crafts furniture was made in two very different varieties: there were 'state' items on the one hand, and useful or 'cottage' items on the other. It is the latter

135 Chair designed by Mackmurdo for the Century Guild, c. 1883

136 The artist's wife in the morning room of their house, Knostrop Old Hall, near Leeds. Oil painting by Grimshaw, 1875

which, from the point of view of the furniture-historian, are the most important. The Arts and Crafts Movement, bringing into focus ideas already enunciated by Percier and Fontaine, proclaimed that form must follow function. Halsey Ricardo, partner of the famous Arts and Crafts potter William Frend de Morgan, complained of the defects of existing furniture in an essay published in 1893: 'Take the common chest of drawers as a case in point. Its function is to hold a man's shirts and his clothes, articles of a known and constant size. Why are the drawers not made proportionate to their duty? Why are they so few and so deep that when filled, as they needs must be – they are uneasy to draw out. . . . It can hardly be economy of labour and material that dictates this, for – if so – why is the usual hanging wardrobe made so preposterously tall?'

155

137 The interior of Gimson's cottage at Sapperton in Gloucestershire, 1904

The Arts and Crafts Movement, in fact, stood at an important intellectual and spiritual crossroads. In part it was backward-looking and nostalgic, inclined to opt out of industrial society. The leading *137* Arts and Crafts furniture craftsmen, such as Ernest Gimson and Ernest and Sydney Barnsley, were inclined to retreat from urban contagion to some quiet part of the countryside, renouncing industry as something altogether unimprovable. At the same time they adopted a thoroughly chauvinist and provincial attitude towards their heritage, finding virtue only in the models provided for them by the English country craftsmen of the seventeenth and eighteenth centuries. Yet they were, at the same time, intelligent and thinking men. The Arts and Crafts Movement attracted those who were to some extent at least intellectuals; it broke down the barriers between the artisan and the middle-class theoretician. A not untypical figure was A. Romney Green, a poet and mathematician, who, influenced by Morris, gave

156

up teaching in order to live by the work of his own hands. He is said to have worked out his designs by means of mathematical calculations, rather than on paper.

One immensely important figure in the Arts and Crafts context was Charles Robert Ashbee, founder of the Guild of Handicraft. The Guild based itself first in the East End of London, only later retreating to Chipping Campden in the Cotswolds, a move which proved fatal to its economics. Though the Guild made metalwork, pottery and jewellery in addition to furniture, the latter formed an important part of its production, from its foundation in 1888 to its final dissolution in 1914. Ashbee believed that craft and industry could exist together – he was prepared to abandon what he called the 'intellectual Ludditism' of Ruskin and Morris, meaning blind hostility to the machine – but he felt some kind of guild or cooperative system must be established: 'We find industrial organisation ever screwing down and screwing down, we find the drive severer, the competition keener, we find industrial democracy ever closing in . . . the levelling and uniformity more necessary, more terrible. What becomes of the individual, of what weight is the little human soul upon this dark archangel's scale?'

This was written in 1908, and by 1911 Ashbee's position had developed still further. 'Modern civilization', he wrote, 'rests on machinery, and no system for the endowment, or the encourage-ment, of the teaching of art can be sound that does not recognize this.'

Unlike some of his colleagues, Ashbee was not a chauvinist, and he was rewarded with a good deal of influence and attention abroad. As early as 1897 the Guild of Handicraft was approached by the Grand Duke of Hesse to make the furnishings for his palace in Darmstadt; they were carried out to designs by the architect Mackay Hugh Baillie Scott. Later Josef Hoffmann's workshops, the Wiener Werkstätte, *138* were to be inspired by the example of the Guild. Perhaps the most interesting of all Ashbee's foreign contacts was Frank Lloyd Wright, *139* whom he met in Chicago in 1900. Ten years later Wright stayed with the Ashbees at Chipping Campden, and it was Ashbee who wrote the preface to the second Wasmuth edition of Wright's work, which was responsible for making the American architect known in Europe (the first edition had been expensive and limited). What Ashbee wrote on this occasion has clear links with the ideas proposed by Walter Gropius when he founded the Bauhaus, and shows the way in which the English Arts and Crafts Movement contributed to the whole European movement towards functional design.

Arts and Crafts thinking enjoyed a more spectacular success in the United States than it ever did on its home ground. In some ways, it must be admitted, this success meant a distortion of the original ideals proposed by the founders of the movement. One of those chiefly responsible for popularizing the Arts and Crafts as a decorative style was a remarkable entrepreneur called Gustav Stickley. Stickley, the son of a stonemason and the eldest of six brothers, encountered the teachings of Ruskin while still young, but does not seem to have been affected by them in any practical way, despite the fact that he was a partner in several successful furniture-businesses. In 1898 he made a trip to Europe, in the course of which he met Voysey and other pioneers of design. This persuaded him to abandon the eclectic and colonial reproduction styles he had been making hitherto. At the Grand Rapids furniture exhibition of June 1900, he showed a new line. This, constructed in ultra-simple fashion of plain oak boards, showed strong signs of Arts and Crafts influence. Stickley was not content merely to imitate the Arts and Crafts manner – in 1901 he introduced a semi-cooperative scheme in his own business, calling it United Crafts. This failed to work satisfactorily, and he dropped it in 1904. The year 1901 also saw the start of a much more successful venture, the monthly magazine the *Craftsman*, which became a lively forum for views on current movements in art and architecture, as well as making propaganda for Stickley's own furniture. The Stickley empire continued to expand until 1913, when he overreached himself by buying a large showroom and office-building in Manhattan, at a time when the fortunes of the Arts and Crafts were already declining. His firm went bankrupt in April 1915.

Stickley's own *Craftsman* brand furniture was never very distinguished, and much of it now seems excessively awkward and heavy, though there was a more elegant line, strongly influenced by the Scottish Art Nouveau architect Mackintosh, which went out for a period under the United Crafts label. This was designed not by Stickley but by an obscure architect and draughtsman called Harvey Ellis. The success which *Craftsman* furniture enjoyed throughout the United States – franchises at one time existed from Boston right across the country to Los Angeles – showed the extent of American enthusiasm for the new doctrines. This, strong enough to bring about

138 Chair in white-painted wood designed by
Hoffmann for the Cabaret Fledermaus, 1907

139 Armchair designed by Wright, *c.* 1904

140 Oak and leather library table
manufactured by Stickley

an apparently unnatural fusion between the mass-marketing of furniture and Ruskinian doctrines of 'honest craftsmanship', also led to a huge upsurge of craft activity among non-professionals. At a grass-roots level, the Arts and Crafts Movement probably affected American society more than it did English, since it appealed so profoundly to the American tradition of self-help.

The English Aesthetic and Arts and Crafts Movements both made a contribution to the rise of Art Nouveau. Basically Art Nouveau was a revolt against nineteenth-century historicism. Its roots lay partly in Aestheticism, and partly in Aestheticism's opposite, the florid Naturalistic style of the first half of the century. These conflicting elements were brought into harmony through the influence of Symbolism. Forms copied from nature, plant forms in particular, were the basic elements used by most Art Nouveau designers, though not by the only really distinguished one to flourish on British soil. This was the Scotsman, Mackintosh, architect of the Glasgow School of Art. The furniture designed by Mackintosh is extremely distinctive. It tends to be exaggeratedly elongated, sometimes painted black, and at other times enamelled white. Splats and supports are pierced with small openings, and there is restrained decoration in a Celtic style, sometimes incised, in the manner of the art furniture of the 1880s, and sometimes made of opaque coloured glass, which was applied with great effect to some of the white enamelled pieces.

Continental Art Nouveau was not well received in England, where it was considered flamboyant and in bad taste, and where, in addition, professionally qualified critics pointed out that the furniture was not 'honestly' constructed. When a group of Art Nouveau pieces were presented to the Victoria and Albert Museum, they were fiercely denounced by prominent members of the English Arts and Crafts Movement.

On the other hand, Mackintosh's work was quite well known and well liked abroad. He showed in the Turin Exhibition of 1902, where extremely advanced work appeared. One of the other exhibitors was the Italian Carlo Bugatti, brother of the sculptor Rembrandt Bugatti and the car-maker Ettore, and forerunner of some of the more freakish designers who appeared in Italy post-1945. Mackintosh's most important foreign link was with the members of the Vienna Secession; Josef Hoffmann visited him in Scotland, and Mackintosh exhibited his furniture in the Eighth Vienna Secession Exhibition and

141 The main bedroom, The Hill House, Dunbartonshire, designed by Mackintosh, 1904

was consulted about the founding of the Wiener Werkstätte. Mackintosh's own late work, done just before and during the First World War, shows reciprocal Viennese influence.

The Wiener Werkstätte were heavily influenced, not merely by Mackintosh, but by English Arts and Crafts ideals. Hoffmann, when formulating the workshop programme, spoke in 1904 of 'a centre of gravity surrounded by the happy noise of handicraft production and welcomed by everybody who truly believes in Ruskin and Morris'. His own creations, though sometimes luxurious, as in the furniture and fittings designed for the Palais Stoclet, Brussels, were carefully restrained, with a strong emphasis on the right angle and on *138* geometrical forms. Though historically part of Art Nouveau, Hoffmann's designs in fact look forward, both to the Art Deco designers of the 1920s (who shared his love of restrained opulence) and to the radical creations of Dè Stijl and the Bauhaus.

Hoffmann's work also has a family likeness to the furniture designed by Wright, whose connection with Ashbee and the English Arts and Crafts Movement has already been mentioned. The most forward-looking aspect of Wright's furniture-designs during the period before 1914 lay not in the forms of the individual pieces, but in his insistence on total unity of effect. 'The most truly satisfactory apartments', he wrote, 'are those in which most or all of the furniture is built in as part of the original scheme. The whole must always be considered as an integral unit.' It seems fitting that the renewed emphasis on built-in furniture (which had existed in one form or another since the middle ages) should have come from the United States, since the Shakers, with their mania for neatness, had already evolved some remarkably efficient designs for furniture of this sort during the first half of the nineteenth century.

The Deutscher Werkbund, founded in 1907, was in many ways akin to the Wiener Werkstätte, but the designers connected with it were far more willing to admit the possibility of fruitful cooperation with industry – thus reflecting the differences between the decaying Austro-Hungarian Empire and the bustling new Germany. The declared objective of the Werkbund was 'the ennoblement of professional work thanks to co-operation between art, industry and manual labour', and it is among those who formed part of it that one discovers the first complete formulation of the concept of industrial design. Their products, tellingly, were at their most adventurous when they were solutions to entirely new problems. Thus, the designs made by the architect Peter Behrens for electric table-lamps now look as if they had been created at least two decades later, towards the end of the 1920s. Behrens's answer to electric light in the home is fascinatingly different from the one supplied by the American designer Louis Comfort Tiffany, whose stained-glass table-lamps and hanging fittings are perhaps the most beautiful ever made. The absence of precedent set both logic and imagination free to do the best they could, and that best was in both cases very impressive.

Tiffany's lamps are among the few fully developed Art Nouveau objects to which the word 'logic' could plausibly be applied. Mackintosh and Hoffmann are Art Nouveau designers only in the most chastened sense, yet even in their work we are often aware of an

162

142 Lamp designed by Tiffany

element of irrationality – for example, in the extreme tallness of the
backs of some of Mackintosh's most typical chairs. Art Nouveau at its
most typical and flamboyant flourished, not in Scotland or Austria,
but in France and Belgium. The marked difference in appearance was
the result of an equally marked difference of approach to the problem
of making furniture. Mackintosh, Hoffmann and some of the
designers of the Deutscher Werkbund produced an intellectual
version of the style, and were part of an argument which leads directly
from Morris & Co. to the Bauhaus. The French designers of the
School of Nancy – the best known are Emile Gallé and Louis
Majorelle – looked in a very different direction. For them, furniture *143*

must have a kind of poetry. Like the paintings of Odilon Redon or Fernand Khnopff, it must lead the spectator into a dream world of half-glimpsed, half-apprehended images. The fact that their furniture often had no kind of constructional logic worried them not at all, though they insisted on the fine finish which would appeal to their prosperous clientele. One of the things which linked what they did to 117 the Naturalistic style and even to the early nineteenth-century rococo revival was an emphasis on voluptuous curves and low-slung comfort: things at the furthest remove from the spikiness of Mackintosh. Art Nouveau of this kind appealed even in Italy, which of all countries was most reluctant to abandon the standard commercial forms of the mid nineteenth century. In remote, conservative Sicily, stunning Art Nouveau interiors were created by Ernesto Basile, with woodwork very close in style to Gallé and Majorelle.

In Belgium perhaps the most original designer of Art Nouveau 145 furniture was Henri van de Velde, who took up a position somewhere

143 'Nénuphar' writing-table in mahogany and ormolu, designed by Majorelle, 1902

144 Edwardian 'Adam'. Bedroom designed by H. Pringuer Benn from H. P. Shapland's *Style Schemes in Antique Furnishings*, 1909

between that adopted by Hoffmann and his colleagues in Vienna and that favoured by the School of Nancy. His dictum was: 'To conceive reasonably is new and ancient simultaneously: it leads to extremes, not to the tried and true.' Following his own maxim, he often produced furniture which seems stranger and more astonishing, though also far more austere, than anything imagined by his French colleagues.

The wide variety of decorative styles created during the second half of the nineteenth century may make it seem as if this were essentially a period of rapid innovation. In one way this is true. An immense amount of creative thought and energy went into both furniture itself and the other decorative arts, and the Arts and Crafts Movement in particular raised these to a new level of consideration, on a par with the 'fine' arts, painting and sculpture. But these innovations must be seen against a background which is often forgotten, because it is so much less interesting to the historian. Every innovative style had to

145 Padouk (Burmese sandalwood) armchair by Van de Velde, with upholstery in cotton batik by Prikker, 1898–99

face fierce competition from eclectic revivals, from copies, and from the antique. Ashbee, for example, despairingly denounced the competition his workmen faced, both from the furniture of the past, and from the copyists of his own day. Even where people did not demand an exact copy of the furniture of the past (assuming that they could not find or could not afford the genuine originals) they settled for some kind of comforting paraphrase. The London furnishing-house Maples, for example, had a great success with a version of *144* Adam, particularly for bedroom furniture, where no piece corresponded with an eighteenth-century original, but all were nevertheless spiced with recognizably Adamesque ornaments and details. In Germany, the renaissance style was subjected to a similar *128* process of bastardization, while in France Louis Seize Impératrice continued its career in increasingly fanciful variations.

166

Just before the outbreak of the First World War, however, there was another recognizable step forward. This was due to the impact made on decoration by Diaghilev's Ballets Russes. The Oriental ballet *Schéhérézade*, first danced in the second Diaghilev season of 1910, had an immense impact both on fashionable dress and fashionable decoration. This was reinforced by *Thamar* two years later. Decor *à la Schéhérézade* was to be fashionable until well into the 1920s – Martine, the decorating firm which belonged to the great couturier Paul Poiret, specialized in interiors of this sort. The emphasis has hitherto been on the great impact the Ballets Russes had on colour, bringing in a taste for purple, jade-green and orange, instead of the pale pastel shades previously fashionable. What has been overlooked is its equally powerful influence on the forms of seat-furniture. Divans had been acceptable in the mock-Moorish interiors the Victorians often

146

146 Bedroom designed by Poiret's decorating firm, Martine, *c.* 1924

used as smoking-rooms, but now huge, shapeless sofas and floor-cushions came into vogue, the forerunners of a great deal of post-1950 seat-furniture. They were doubly significant because they brought with them a new attitude to manners, and indeed to the body. Now it was permissible to sprawl and loll, where formerly it was necessary to sit upright.

Another innovation just before the war, though less important, is nevertheless worth mentioning. This is the rise of the the professional decorator. It has been said that the person who invented the concept of interior decoration as we know it today was the novelist Edith Wharton, who started her career as a writer by collaborating with Ogden Cookman on a volume called *The Decoration of Houses*, which was published in 1897. She preached a cautious, sensible good taste, albeit on rather a grand scale, which has been the stock-in-trade of most professional decorators ever since. The first person to practise decorating as a profession was the ex-actress Elsie de Wolfe, who survived to publish her memoirs, entitled *After All*, as late as 1935. In this book she describes how she carried out the commission which made her reputation: the decoration of the new Colony Club in New York in 1905. The Colony Club was in its way a revolutionary undertaking: 'It was to be conducted on the same lines as a men's club and was to be a retreat where women could go as men go to their clubs for relaxation and entertainment.' As such, it aroused an immense amount of interest. Miss de Wolfe's decorations, fresh, simple and practical, with a lavish use of chintz, hitherto more or less confined to bedrooms, were hugely influential. The Colony Club was a feminist enterprise, and the decorator used it as an opportunity to make a feminist statement, a fact of which she seems to have been perfectly well aware. Though homes had always been regarded as the province of women, it was only now that women asserted an absolute right to decide what would go into them. Vanbrugh, at the beginning of the eighteenth century, had had a number of battles with the redoubtable Sarah, Duchess of Marlborough, about the interior arrangements of Blenheim. On the whole she lost them. Houses had often been eclectic before, filled with the possessions of different generations. But it took the rise of the decorator to make eclecticism into a principle, so that an interior became a collage, balancing the claims of personality and practicality, making use of what was available rather than inventing something new to replace it.

CHAPTER NINE

1914–1942

The development of furniture and decoration in the period between the two World Wars is still not completely in focus from the historical point of view, despite a spate of recent publications concerned with Art Deco. These publications are, of course, connected with the fashionable post-war revival of Deco on the part of both designers and decorators. Although Bevis Hillier, in his pioneering book *Art Deco*, published in 1968, described this as being 'the last of the total styles', in fact there always existed various alternatives to it, even when the fashion was at its height. The story of the decorative arts in the period 1920–40 is at least as complicated as in the late Victorian and Edwardian period, and has, in addition, been far less thoroughly investigated. Nevertheless, it is possible to come to certain basic conclusions, and to divide the material into a number of broad groupings.

1. Luxury Deco – an aristocratic and fashionable style, still with many links with the nineteenth and even the eighteenth century. This flourished chiefly in France, and the 1920s rather than the 1930s were its heyday, since it was then badly affected by the world economic crisis.

2. A vulgarization of Deco for the mass-market, sometimes shading off into what the caricaturist and architectural historian Osbert Lancaster describes as 'Modernistic'.

3. International Modern – furniture designed mostly by leading avant-garde architects. At first the main centres of activity were Weimar Germany and also France. Later, with the rise of the dictatorships, experimental activity shifted to the United States.

4. A somewhat tempered and compromised continuation of Arts and Crafts ideals, visible in Britain, and also in Scandinavia, where the 1930s saw the development of a very recognizable local style, sometimes labelled 'Swedish Modern'.

5. Reactionary historicism. This could take many forms, ranging from the boldly theatrical effects contrived by leading interior

decorators – Elsie de Wolfe and her rivals and successors – to the cheap 'Tudorbethan' furniture produced in England for the mass-market.

These categories are by no means watertight, and there are many overlappings and traces of reciprocal influence.

Art Deco takes its name from an exhibition held in Paris in 1925, 'L'Exposition Internationale des Arts Décoratifs et Industriels Modernes'. This was certainly responsible, as Hillier says, for presenting the style to the world as something obviously new. Nevertheless it remains arguable that some of the leading Deco furniture-designers had already produced their finest work by the time the exhibition took place.

In fashionable circles Deco influences were already making themselves felt in the years which immediately preceded the First World War. There is a distinctly Deco look to some of the furniture produced to Hoffmann's designs, for example – a sumptuous restraint which announces the end of the wilder excesses of Art Nouveau. In France, Art Deco can be seen as having developed out of Art Nouveau in much the same way that the Louis XVI style developed out of the rococo of Louis XV. The comparison is reinforced by the fact that the best French Deco furniture shows many traces of Louis XVI and even of Empire influence. The most typical Art Deco interiors of the first half of the 1920s combined Russian ballet colourings with furniture adapted from Directoire and Empire models. The adaptation usually involved bringing the seats of chairs and sofas much nearer to the ground, with a consequent readjustment of proportions, including a heightening of the backs. Because seats were lower, low tables were required, and Art Deco is really responsible for the birth of the cocktail table. These low tables echoed another influence – they were often based on Oriental models, and in general there was a strong Chinese influence in much good Art Deco, with a particular liking for lacquer. In general, the leading Art Deco cabinet-makers preferred very luxurious materials. All kinds of exotic woods were in favour, ranging from the very light to the very dark. Trimmings were in ivory and in shagreen. This latter material, pale green with an intricate scale pattern to imitate sharkshin, became one of the hallmarks of the best Art Deco cabinet-making. Some cabinet-makers, such as Jean-François Leleu, also experimented with mother-of-pearl inlays. In order to show off the fine materials available, Art

147 Drawing-room designed by Ruhlmann and shown at the 1925 'Exposition des Arts Décoratifs', Paris

148 Cabinet in macassar ebony inlaid with ivory, by Ruhlmann

Deco furniture usually had smooth, plain surfaces. Tables, especially dining-tables, were made with a single massive central pillar, instead of four or six legs. Both for convenience and for unity of effect, a great deal of furniture, especially bedroom furniture, was built in.

Despite this concession to modernity, luxury Art Deco furniture was in general thoroughly conservative. It invented a few new furniture-types – the cocktail cabinet as well as the cocktail table – and altered details, such as the proportions of seat-furniture. But essentially it restated the old ideals of fine craftsmanship, and made no pretence that it was intended for other than the few. With this kind of Deco, one always has to make the distinction between radical innovation, which is extremely rare, and a liking for superficial novelty. Occasionally, for example, one finds Deco designers making symbolic use of 'modern' materials, such as chrome, but they never bother to press these experiments very far. The most typical of the French Deco cabinet-makers was Emile-Jacques Ruhlmann, whose

148

work easily equalled the technical standards set by his eighteenth-century predecessors, and in some respects, such as the fit of drawers, actually surpassed them. More experimental in their approach were men like Pierre Legrain and Marcel Coard. Both occasionally made furniture inspired by African art, and in particular by African stools *149* and chairs in carved wood. These pieces echoed the interest in ethnographical art which had first surfaced before the war, with the paintings of Picasso's 'Negro' period.

If Deco was in many respects a conservative style, the clients who commissioned the best Deco pieces were not, in the early and middle 1920s, a particularly conservative group. The old aristocratic clientele which had survived to some extent right up to the outbreak of the First World War was now replaced by another, more ephemeral group. The great Paris couturiers and couturières, such as Jacques *150* Doucet and Jeanne Lanvin, were enthusiasts for the style, and so were people who were successful in the theatre. The Slump hit private patronage of this sort rather hard, and though Deco continued its development during the 1930s, it was now as an official manifestation. The public rooms of the French liner *Normandie* were, in particular, a *152* monument to what the Deco designers could still do, but their work grew visibly heavier and more pompous as a result of the change of patronage.

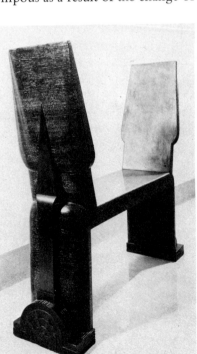

149 African-influenced stool made by Legrain for Doucet

The popular Deco style was far more widespread geographically, and penetrated much further down the social scale than luxury Deco. The influences that went to create it were more various than those that affected the great Parisian designers. One influence, felt more in textiles and wallpapers than in furniture, was that of Cubism and Futurism. They inspired the angular abstract patterns that earned this aspect of Deco the nickname 'Jazz Modern'. In addition, there were two sets of influences from non-European cultures. One was a neo-Egyptian vogue, triggered by the opening of the tomb of Tutankhamun in 1922. This displayed itself chiefly in small objects and in jewellery. The other was the so-called Aztec style, inspired partly by novels, in particular D. H. Lawrence's *The Plumed Serpent*, published in 1926, and partly by the search for native American motifs. This search was motivated in turn by the growth of American chauvinism in the years of disillusion that followed the war, but this did not prevent the Aztec style from crossing the Atlantic. The most obvious borrowing from pre-Columbian art made by the popular Deco designers was their adaptation of the stepped shape of the Aztec pyramid. This appears often in case-furniture, and most frequently of all in those pieces with specifically contemporary associations, such as cocktail cabinets and wireless sets. It was also popular for clocks. *151* Wireless-set design has recently been made the theme of specialized exhibitions, as these objects, meeting an entirely new need, often expressed the contemporary spirit with an inventive lack of self-

150 (*opposite*) Interior designed by Gray for the modiste Suzanne Talbot, 1919–22

151 Pye Twin Triple portable battery radio, 1930

152 (*below*) The *Grand Salon* of the liner *Normandie*, 1935

consciousness reminiscent of the best designs for electric lamps created previous to 1914. One favourite motif, considered by association especially suitable for the purpose, was the zigzag lightning-flash device which was to become one of the most typical emblems of the 1930s, and which was to acquire a sinister resonance through its association with Hitler's SS.

Popular Deco design was at best rather uncontrolled and at worst degenerated into the Modernistic anti-style defined with deadly accuracy by Lancaster in his *Homes Sweet Homes* as 'a nightmare amalgam of a variety of elements derived from several sources. The foundation was provided by that Jazz style which enjoyed a

mercifully brief period of popularity in the immediately post-Versailles period, which was itself the fruit of a fearful union between the flashier side of Ballets Russes and a hopelessly vulgarized version of Cubism. To this were added elements derived from the *style colonial* popularized by the Paris Exhibition of 1927, such as an all too generous use of the obscure and more hideous woods, and a half-hearted simplicity that derived from a complete misunderstanding of the Corbusier-Gropius school of architects and found uneasy expression in unvarnished wood and chromium plate, relentlessly misapplied.'

The 'Corbusier-Gropius school' here referred to was that part of the Modern Movement which applied its theories to the decorative as well as the fine arts. The Modern Movement itself goes back to the first decade of the century, with the appearance of the Fauves at the Salon d'Automne in 1905 and the publication of the First Futurist Manifesto in 1909. But since Modernism had been a reaction against Symbolist totality, it at first took very little interest in such things as furniture. Yet the materials for a new theory were already lying at hand.

The functionalist concept was already latent by 1900. By that time the German architect Richard Riemerschmid was capable of designing chairs which, in their practicality, lightness and simplicity, strike us as being in the functionalist mainstream. The earliest furniture actually to align itself with one of the main tendencies in modern art was, however, that designed by a member of the Dutch De Stijl group, Gerrit Thomas Rietveld, in 1919. The abstract geometric forms that appear in the paintings of Mondrian are here translated without compromise into the sphere of the decorative arts, and the result is furniture which is stringent in the extreme, deliberately purged of all decorative accretions. The next step was to be taken at the Bauhaus, which was founded at Weimar in the same year that Rietveld made his designs, and subsequently moved to Dessau and then to Berlin. The Bauhaus, so far as the decorative arts were concerned, at first had an Arts and Crafts orientation, but in 1924 this changed to a far more positive emphasis on the idea of collaboration with industry. The essence of mature Bauhaus doctrine is expressed in a statement made by its founder, Gropius: 'In order to create something that functions properly – a container, a chair, a house – its essence has to be explored; for it should serve its purpose to

176

perfection, i.e. it should fulfil its function practically and be durable, inexpensive and "beautiful".'

Perhaps the most important furniture-designers associated with the Bauhaus were the two architects, Marcel Breuer and Mies van der Rohe. Breuer was the more prolific in creating designs for furniture. *154* In the 1920s both men explored the possibilities offered by metal construction, thus taking up an idea which had first been tried out in the mid nineteenth century. In this connection Breuer made a statement which is of particular interest. 'Metal furniture', he wrote, in an essay published in 1928, 'is part of a modern room. It is "styleless", for it is expected not to express any particular styling beyond its purpose and the construction necessary theretofore.'

He also added, with reference to his own designs: 'I purposely chose metal for this furniture in order to achieve the characteristics of modern space elements. . . . The heavy, imposing stuffing of a comfortable chair has been replaced by a tightly fitted fabric and some light, springy pipe brackets. The steel used, and particularly the aluminium, are remarkably light, though they withstand severe static strain (tractive stress of the material). The light shape increases the flexibility. All types are constructed from the same standardized elementary parts which may be taken apart or exchanged at any time. This metal furniture is intended to be nothing but a necessary apparatus for contemporary life.'

If, as Le Corbusier once claimed, a house was 'a machine for living in', then for Breuer a chair was a machine for sitting on. Yet the chairs he designed do not bear out his claim to be completely neutral. They now seem like the aggressive statement of a certain set of design principles, as moralistic in their way as Pugin's designs for Gothic furniture.

Perhaps the most original aspect of this metal furniture designed by Mies and Breuer is its employment of the cantilever principle in order to combine strength and lightness. Mies designed a remarkably elegant cantilever chair in 1926, and Breuer followed with a better- *155* balanced and more practical one two years later.

The innovations they proposed did in fact make some headway with ordinary commercial furniture-manufacturers. In the 1930s, for example, the English firm of Pel took to making steel furniture after *156* two of the directors of the steel-tube manufacturer Accles & Pollock had seen some examples of Bauhaus work in the then new Strand

153 Rietveld, painted wood sideboard, 1919

154 Wassily chair by Breuer, 1925

155 Cantilever chair designed by Mies van der Rohe, 1926

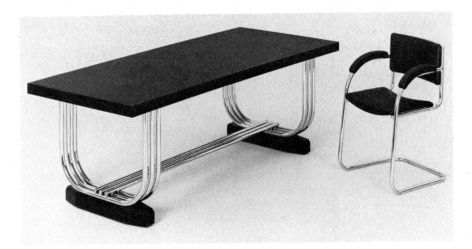

156 Pel tubular steel furniture. English, 1930s

157 'Le grand confort' chair designed by Le Corbusier, 1928

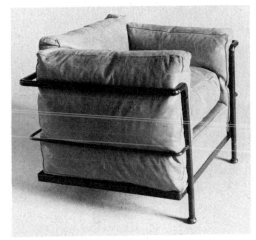

158 Armchair 406 in bent and laminated birch, designed by Aalto

159 Laminated wood stacking chairs designed by Aalto, 1929–30

Palace Hotel in London. Demand for steel tube was low, and they thought something similar would provide a new outlet for their product. Pel furniture came into being in 1931, and the firm's productions were extensively used in Broadcasting House, London, then in the throes of completion.

Yet it is also surprising how far furniture of this kind remained a luxurious minority taste. Some of it, indeed, was designed so that matters could not be otherwise. Perhaps the most famous of all Bauhaus furniture designs was Mies's steel-and-leather chair created for the German pavilion at the Barcelona Exhibition of 1929. With its sweeping curves of chromium steel, it became a kind of symbol of the whole Modern Movement; it is still in production today. Yet it is neither cheap to make nor suitable for mass production.

For all the designers' assertions that they abhorred the idea of style, International Modern furniture quickly created its own stylistic category. This is as visible in France, in the furniture designed by Le Corbusier in collaboration with Charlotte Perriand, by Eileen Gray, and by Robert Mallet-Stevens, as it is in Germany. Le Corbusier's furniture was troublesome to manufacture and sometimes uncomfortable to use, though often extremely elegant to look at. If Breuer and Mies's most striking technical contribution was the cantilever 157 chair, Le Corbusier's was a form of armchair with large cushions fitted into a metal framework. The shifting of the skeleton from the inside to the outside of a piece of upholstered furniture was a prophetic act, as furniture made in the last two decades has shown.

Metal furniture, often in ugly and unimaginative forms, soon established itself for use outside the home, particularly in offices. The lack of emotional associations which enthusiasts for the modern saw as one of its chief virtues prevented it from being used where it might otherwise have been welcome. Few people found it sympathetic in a domestic context, at least outside the kitchen. For this and other reasons modern architect-designers tended to shift their attention during the 1930s from metal to laminated wood. Breuer himself, exiled from Germany by Hitler's rise to power, designed a range of laminated wood furniture for the English firm of Isokon. This dates from 1935. The most famous designer of laminated wood furniture 158 was the Finnish architect Alvar Aalto. Aalto took ideas which had originally been pioneered by Thonet, and developed them in harmony with the established principles of modern design. His

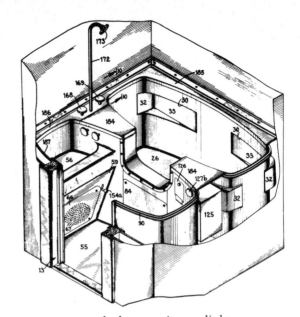

160 Patent drawing of Dymaxion bathroom by Buckminster Fuller, 1938

furniture found a ready acceptance not merely because it was light and practical, but because it was cheap. His stacking chairs and stools, *159* designed *c.* 1930, became what one might call 'invisible modernism', and found their way via bathroom, nursery and kitchen into environments otherwise hostile to all forms of modern art.

The development of cheap and reliable plywoods, blockboards and laminated boards was one of the chief technical advances of the decade before the Second World War. The other, derived from experiments made in the automobile industry, was foam-rubber upholstery. These advances had much greater significance for the future than the recapitulation, during the 1920s, of Victorian experiments with metal. But neither was an entirely unmixed blessing. Plywood and other kinds of near-wood not only offered an alternative to frame-and-panel construction; they also made it possible to put a large part of the furniture-industry on a fully industrial basis, and the results, in lesser hands than those of Aalto and Breuer, were often far from happy.

One important development in the 1930s was the way in which architects began to think of certain rooms as capsules, in which architecture, furniture and function were completely integrated. The most extreme, and most famous, example of this tendency was Buckminster Fuller's Dymaxion bathroom unit. Designed in 1938, *160*

181

this was the first entirely prefabricated 'appliance room'. Bathrooms were particularly susceptible to this kind of treatment not only because they were essentially service areas but because they, like wireless sets on their own smaller scale, had no real prehistory, and so could be looked at with an entirely unprejudiced eye by designer and client alike. Modernism – even extreme Modernism – in a bathroom offended nobody.

If Aalto and Breuer employed wood in a visibly industrial fashion, there were also other furniture-designers who were prepared to try to use it in a contemporary way, while still retaining some kind of *161* foothold in the past. In England, Ambrose Heal and Gordon Russell contrived to bring over some part of the Arts and Crafts tradition and reconcile it with ordinary commercial practice. The firm of Betty Joel was also responsible for excellent joiner-made furniture in teak and oak. This firm also made use of the new 'Empire' woods – Queensland walnut, Indian laurel, Australian silky oak, Indian greywood. These gave a contemporary accent to quite conservative designs because the colour, texture and pattern were unfamiliar.

The real credit for pioneering a new attitude towards traditional joinery belongs to the leading Scandinavian designers of the 1930s.

161 Illustration from a Heal's furniture catalogue, March 1913

162 Detail of Queen Mary's doll's house, 1924

Prominent among them were Carl Malmsten of Sweden – whose career began as early as 1916, when he won a contract for the decoration of the new Stockholm Town Hall – and Kaare Klint of Denmark. Scandinavian furniture reflected not only the local craft tradition, which was a good deal less self-conscious than its English equivalent, but the Scandinavian life-style – consciously democratic and unpretentious. Scandinavian furniture was invariably practical furniture, unobtrusive and easy to live with. To these qualities it owed a steady and long-lasting success.

Scandinavian taste lay almost at the opposite extreme from that of the much-talked-of decorators who worked for an ultra-fashionable clientele in England, France and America, and the fact that the two could coexist illustrates the contradictory nature of the period. The people who employed these decorators often had almost no interest in the contemporary arts. So far as they understood them, they tended to dislike them. Sometimes their ideas were almost purely conservative, and what they required was a sensible reinterpretation of period styles. This taste at its grandest is reflected in the furniture and fittings of Queen Mary's doll's house. But often such people had *162*

183

a strong interest in what struck them as novel and fashionable. The more restless were willing to redecorate their houses almost as often as they renewed their wardrobes. The decoration of houses became, in these fortunate circles, a recognized means of self-expression – the Walpoles, Beckfords, and Ludwigs of Bavaria were admired exemplars. The norm of fashionable decoration (in so far as anything so volatile could have a norm) was for a long while the manner which Lancaster called 'Curzon Street Baroque', an eclectic reinterpretation

163 of the eighteenth century somewhat influenced by artists such as James Pryde and Rex Whistler.

As Lancaster says: 'Gone were the Louis Seize chairs and the Largillière portraits, and their place was taken by innumerable pieces of hand-painted furniture from Venice and an abundant supply of both the Canalettos. At the same time a markedly ecclesiastical note is struck by the forests of twisted baroque candlesticks, willingly surrendered by countless Italian padres (in exchange for the wherewithal with which to purchase up-to-date machine-turned brass electroliers), old leather hymn books cunningly hollowed out to receive cigarettes, and exuberant *prie-dieu* ingeniously transformed into receptacles for gramophone records.'

Decorators in the top flight often had a name for personal

164 specialities. Syrie Maugham, for example, was famous for her off-white rooms, with fumed and pickled furniture. Her own Villa Elisa

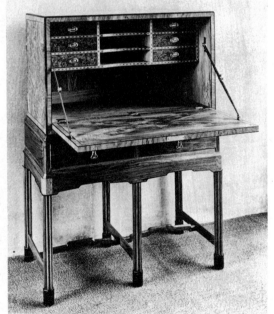

163 Fall-front writing-cabinet designed by Russell, 1927

164 Syrie Maugham's
drawing-room at 213
King's Road, Chelsea, as
illustrated in *The Studio*,
February 1933

at Le Touquet, as described in *House & Garden* in 1927, had a drawing-room done entirely in tones of beige, except for peach-coloured silk curtains.

Maugham's work, in turn, was probably one of the prime sources of inspiration for Hollywood set-designers, who showed their audiences a lush never-never land of mirrors, pale silk or leather sofas, white satin drapes and polar-bear-skin rugs. The monochrome manner, of course, ideally suited films which were shot in black-and-white. But female stars also adopted it for their own, and transferred it *165* to the houses they actually inhabited, sometimes with a touch of Spanish renaissance thrown in. The films themselves, and the

165 Marlene Dietrich at home in Beverly Hills, early 1930s

publicity photographs given out by the studios, gave the mass public something to dream about amid the miseries of the Slump, and established an image of glamour which has proven stubbornly durable. One reason for its success, in addition to lavish vicarious luxury, is a touch-me-not quality; these interiors are so marvellously, so outrageously impractical that they become the democratic equivalent for the equally impractical setting Beckford created for himself at Fonthill. They made a sad contrast with the kind of interior which the average movie-goer of the 1930s probably lived in.

It was during this period that mass-produced furniture reached its nadir, in terms both of quality and of design. The gap between the best and the worst was never more pronounced in any epoch, and it is just this aspect that the current romanticization of the period tends to pass over in silence.

CHAPTER TEN

1942–the present

The rapid technological development that affected furniture during
the 1930s became more rapid still in the 1950s, 1960s and 1970s. In
terms of the materials and techniques used to produce it, furniture has
moved further and faster in the past thirty years than in the three
centuries between 1500 and 1800. Technical advance has been
accompanied, as in the early Victorian period, by marked stylistic
uncertainty.

The war years affected the furniture-industry drastically in Europe,
while leaving it relatively untouched in America. In England, for
example, the most significant result of the war was the introduction of
the Utility Furniture Scheme in 1942. This imposed complete
standardization of design, in an effort to provide enough furniture

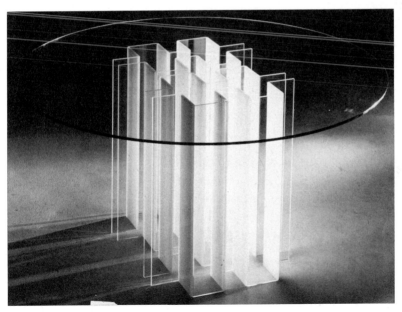

166 Deco Revival. Ziggurat dining-table designed by Quadrant 4

167 Utility furniture, designed by a panel under the chairmanship of Russell, 1942

either for those who were setting up house because they were newly married, or replacing possessions lost when they were bombed out. Utility was a compromise between the Arts and Crafts spirit and mass-production techniques and materials. Its forms had the puritan 137 plainness beloved of designers working in the tradition of Gimson and the Barnsleys; the materials included substitutes which such craftsmen would never have accepted. There is now a tendency amongst historians of design to see Utility as a great reform of public taste, a purge which got rid of many of the excesses of the 1930s. If so, it was a reform which was much resented, and a rebellion against it was to take place as soon as conditions allowed. The adoption of the extravagant New Look in women's clothes after the war is a parallel case. Nevertheless, Utility left behind it a considerable legacy, and did much to break down consumer resistance to modern design. Much of the furniture produced in Britain during the 1950s, even after restrictions were gradually eased, still owed a great deal to the original 167 Utility range, some designs for which were produced by a Design Panel, under the chairmanship of Russell.

188

As horizons widened, it was possible to see that 'respectable' modern design had now split into at least three main traditions – American, Scandinavian and Italian – each owing something very important to the environment that fostered it. The one that owed most to the Bauhaus was the one that had its roots in America. But what the Bauhaus had achieved was now being developed by native American designers, prominent among them Charles Eames, and with the help of the formidable resources of American technology. To already standard metal and plywood American designers added glass fibre reinforced plastic. Significant milestones in its use were Eames's DAR chair of 1948, and Eero Saarinen's Eomb Chair 70MC *168* of 1945–48. Both of these used plastic to create multi-curved baroque forms with their own brand of ergonomic and technological logic. These would have been tabu among an earlier generation of architect-designers even if they had possessed the means to achieve them. In a way, the American style involved a love-affair with industry. American designs seemed to assert that the designer in close day-to-day alliance with the latest technology could always do better than one who restricted himself to occasional collaboration with it. The tendency continued throughout the 1950s and 1960s and culminated in objects such as the Tulip chairs designed by Saarinen for Knoll. *169* These cast aside any hint of the old alliance with craft – they are pure statements of form, born from the designer's brain and the capabilities of the machine.

Scandinavian furniture continued to fulfil quite naturally many of *170* the demands made by the new age. The social tendencies which had gone towards its creation in the 1930s were strengthening rather than diminishing. But the leading Scandinavian designers, such as Arne Jacobsen, were perfectly willing to move with the times, and were by no means indifferent to the new technology. Jacobsen's Swan chair, *172* designed in 1958, is fully as advanced in its way as anything produced in America. Yet it also invites a reference to something much nearer home. Though less stark, it is obviously related to the furniture that Aalto designed in the 1930s.

The most unexpected contender for design leadership was Italy, yet furniture-design experienced a strong revival here after the war, *173* despite the long hiatus imposed by Fascism. In fact, Fascist censorship of design and architecture had never been as thorough-going in Italy as Nazi control in Germany, and a number of genuinely meritorious

189

168 DAR chair designed by Eames, 1948   169 Tulip chair designed by Saarinen, 1953

170 Stainless-steel and canework chair with red goatskin cushion, designed by Poul Kjaerholm, 1965

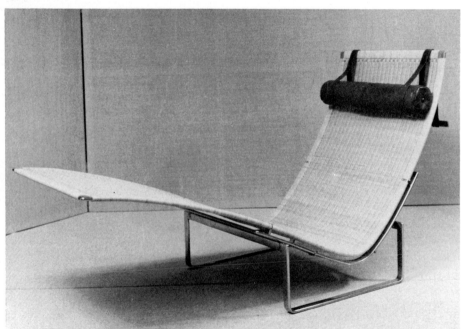

171 Antelope chair by Race, designed for the Festival of Britain, 1951

172 Swan chair designed by Jacobsen, 1958

173 Chairs designed by Bertoia

things had been built under Mussolini. Typically, because of the Duce's imperial ambitions, the idiom was a kind of stripped-down classicism, only a step away from true functionalism, and the grander kind of Italian furniture tended to go the same way in the 1930s, taking ideas from the neo-classical side of French Art Deco.

The war, if it did not do Italian arms much credit, did stimulate Italian technical ingenuity. Some Italian post-war design, such as a folding canvas chair on a butterfly framework, derived directly from campaign furniture provided for the Italian armies. What counted most after 1945, however, was the sense of liberation. It provided a catalyst for the Italian consciousness of style, and the daring quality of the Italian imagination. Like the coachwork provided by leading Italian coachbuilders such as Pininfarina, Italian designers approached all problems of function totally without preconceptions. They also had a sense of line, colour and luxury which was sometimes lacking among their competitors.

Compared with the efforts of American, Scandinavian and Italian designers, British work was somewhat provincial. Yet, as the Festival of Britain showed in 1951, a real effort was being made by British designers to catch up with the Modern Movement. The chair designed by Ernest Race for general use on the Festival site, with its framework of steel rods and moulded plywood seat, looks somewhat prim compared to American achievements in the same idiom, but it was nevertheless committed to the new age.

Looking through the booklet *Design in the Festival* issued in connection with the exhibition, one is struck by the mannerism of many of the designs, with their splayed legs and dished wooden knobs. The television and wireless sets are particularly clumsy, and the latter have none of the exuberance of their predecessors in the 1930s.

However, 'good' design was only part of the story in the fifteen years that followed the war. There was also *kitsch* – a kind of bad taste which was becoming assertive about its own right to exist. *Kitsch* had not yet become a cult, but was already achieving an identity. Sometimes it revealed itself even in the work of well-respected modern designers. Because of the hiatus imposed by the war, the late 1940s and the 1950s turned at this popular level into a stylistic battleground. There was a definite revolt against rectilinear forms, even when the material chosen did not impose such a change. It can be

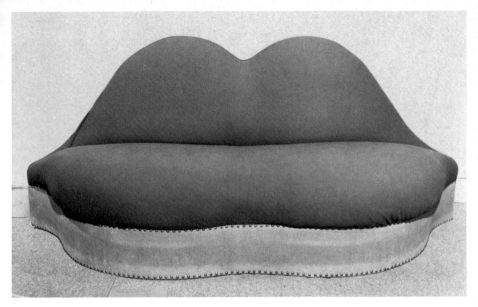

174 Mae West Hot Lips Sofa, based on a painting by Salvador Dalí, 1936–37

detected in furniture from many countries. Amoeboid shapes, apparently derived from the wooden reliefs of the surrealist sculptor Jean Arp, but also (so Hillier asserts) from the amorphous blotches favoured by wartime camouflage designers, became widely popular. These shapes appear in immediately post-war furniture by the French designer Jean Royère, and also in Swedish free-form coffee-tables of the same date. Another popular motif was the boomerang. It was particularly favoured by a group of leading Italian designers, among them Carlo Mollino and Enrico Rava, who were the leaders in the post-war Italian revival.

Among other typically 1950s motifs identified by Hillier in his book *Austerity/Binge* are the flying-saucer shape, the cocktail-cherry-on-a-stick (taken partly, he thinks, from models of atomic structures), and the trellis pattern. The last goes back at least as far as de Wolfe, who did a trellised interior in the Colony Club; but the other two have scientific, even science-fiction overtones, and were used as symbols of commitment to the future.

Much further down the scale of 1950s design were the artefacts spawned by the new Rock culture. Rock had hardly as yet begun to affect the appearance of objects outside its own specialized field – it

175   made the juke-box, for example, into a kind of chromium-plated altar to Elvis Presley and his peers – but it was full of significance for the future, when Pop Art would be the ruling style in painting, and when the Pop influence would spread to interior decoration as well.

The 1960s and 1970s marked the growth of a much keener stylistic self-consciousness. A wide range of choices was now available to anyone interested in modern design. Some – though this is not a complete list – can be enumerated as follows:

1. Classic Modern. Designs by Mies, Breuer and Le Corbusier no longer manufactured were brought back into the repertoire. To these were added others, some by contemporary 'name' designers, such as Eames, Saarinen and Harry Bertoia, while some were 'proto-modern' classics, such as Victorian steel rocking-chairs and Thonet bentwood furniture.

2. Radical Modern. This embraced not only new technological advances, but new attitudes towards interior architecture.

3. Package Modern. Not merely furniture sold in knock-down form, but department-store marketing of a total contemporary 'look'.

4. Pop. Furniture and decoration related to 1960s Pop Art.

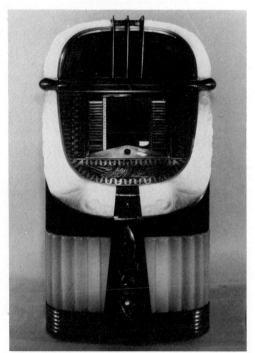

175 Ami 'A' juke-box, 1946–48

176 Interior by Aram Designs, London, 1970s

5. Deco Revival, sometimes also labelled Retro.
6. Post Modern. A commercial idiom, which neither embraced Modernism wholeheartedly nor completely rejected it, but which favoured instead a stylistic amalgam, with modern or modernistic elements used quite empirically. This was the mid twentieth-century version of a phenomenon which has occurred at all periods but which in the 1970s acquired a kind of academic respectability of its own.

Many of these styles, like the conflicting decorative idioms of the inter-war period, tended to overlap.

Classic Modern was an unabashedly luxurious style, which *176* expressed a confidence that the Modern Movement in art had now established itself on a level with the other great historical styles. Despite the insistence of the Bauhaus designers that their furniture was essentially styleless, their designs were now seen as having the authority that was also accorded to the furniture of men like Adam, Hope and Percier and Fontaine. These comparisons are deliberately chosen since, as the years went by, the neo-classic basis of Bauhaus design tended to reveal itself more and more. Indeed Mies, in his architectural work, had never denied the influence of the rational neo-classicism of Karl Friedrich von Schinkel, the greatest German architect of the first half of the nineteenth century. Classic Modern

195

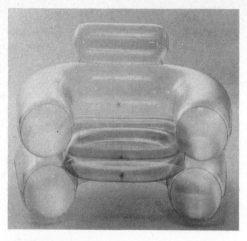

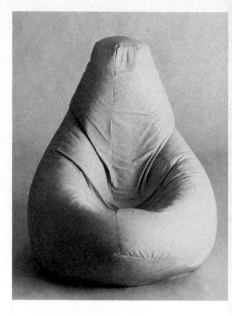

177 Blow chair designed by De Pas, D'Urbino, Lomazzi and Scholari, and produced by Zanotta of Milan in 1967

178 Sacco chair designed by Gatti, Paolini and Teodoro in 1968, and produced by Zanotta of Milan in 1969

179 Le Bibambole sofa designed by Mario Bellini, early 1960s

interiors were arranged to show off the aesthetic qualities of the furniture they contained – the pieces were presented as independent sculptural objects, against great expanses of polished marble or wood. They themselves were manufactured to the highest standards and were in no sense mass-produced. Though the designs retained their impact and relevance, they never succeeded in penetrating the mass-market, as the Bauhaus designers had hoped they would when they came off the drawing-boards in the mid 1920s.

Radical Modern embraced a wide range of technological experiments. Indeed, it is at least arguable that, from the point of view of methods of manufacture and materials, furniture advanced at a more rapid rate during the 1960s than it did during any preceding decade. For various reasons seat-furniture was a particular subject of 179 experiment. One of these reasons, perhaps indeed the most powerful, was a steep rise in manufacturing costs, which tended to raise the price of traditional upholstered furniture to unacceptable levels. Among the more striking innovations were the inflatable Blow chair, by 177 Scholari, D'Urbino, Lomazzi and De Pas; and the Sacco chair by 178 Gatti, Paolini and Teodoro. Both were produced by Zanotta of Milan, in 1967 and 1969 respectively. Though outwardly so different from one another, these chairs had important qualities in common. They were examples of 'provisional' furniture – provisional in shape, provisional even in actual presence. The Blow chair, made of PVC, could be inflated or deflated as required. Sometimes the transparency of the plastic skin emphasized the immaterial nature of the object. The Sacco was not only very light, it completely contradicted Classic Modernism's preference for rigid and, if possible, cubical form. It consisted of a sack filled with plastic granules which adapted itself to the movements of the body. These forms of experimental seating were, however, in the last resort less comfortable than the upholstered furniture they aimed to replace, and established themselves only for a time. A longer-lasting and more significant success went to chairs and sofas of more conventional form which were made of expanded plastic foam encased in a fitted cover. These were much cheaper than conventional upholstery with a rigid frame and springs encased in webbing, and were not all that much inferior in comfort and durability.

Radical Modernism also concerned itself with the abolition of nearly all movable furniture, of whatever kind. It was no longer a question of simply providing enough built-in storage space to make case-furniture unnecessary. The interior space was now scooped and hollowed to provide places where people could sit. The 'conversation pit', as it was called, first made its appearance in houses designed by Saarinen's architectural partnership during the late 1950s. Later, interior designers such as Max Glendinning had the idea of raising part of the floor-area of a room into a series of stepped platforms where cushions could be placed. These platforms were unified with the rest of the floor by being covered with the same fitted carpeting. In this way some rooms came to resemble the all-embracing environments devised by contemporary Minimal artists.

Sculpture of the 1960s was in any case closely allied to much of the contemporary rigid plastic and metal furniture, and it was even possible to find a resemblance between the Sacco chair and the soft sculptures of an artist such as Robert Morris. The Italian art critic

180 Interior with conversation pit designed by Clyde Rich, 1960s

181 Pastille chair designed by
Aero Aarnio, 1968

Gillo Dorfles, writing in 1969, said: 'Furniture, especially in plastic, is judged by an aesthetic criterion which renders it similar, on the one hand, to the bodywork of a car and industrial objects, and on the other to some of the more recent productions of Minimal Art (primary structures made in sheet-metal and brightly coloured plastic).' The sight of an object like the Pastille chair, a brightly *181* coloured flattened ovoid with a dent in the top to receive the buttocks, conveys the force of the comparison.

What I have labelled Package Modernism has been in a state of continuous development from the mid 1950s to the present day. In England it arrived more suddenly, and therefore was more sharply visible, than in the United States. The first stirrings of Package Modernism were felt in kitchen furniture; fitted kitchens, factory-made but assembled on the spot, were among the more significant innovations of the immediately post-war years. Those of about 1951 had unit furniture made of metal, but this was superseded by wood, wood products and plastics, a change which symbolized the gradual incorporation of the kitchen into the general living-area. Immensely important in the rise of Package Modernism in England were Terence Conran's 'Habitat' retail shops; the first two were opened in 1964, and their declared aim was to put good modern design within the reach of everybody. In fact Habitat, as the chain expanded, did far more than this. It presented a sampling of Classic Modern, Radical Modern and even Retro designs. There was an increasing emphasis, as the mail-order side developed, on furniture which could be sold packed flat, *182* but assembled by the least skilled within moments. In May 1977

199

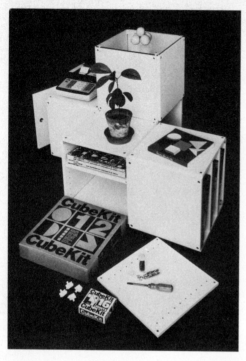

182 Cube-kit furniture designed by
Donald Maxwell, 1976

Design magazine quoted the Habitat furniture-buyer as follows:
'People like to go into a shop on a Saturday afternoon, pick up a chair
in a box, take it away, put it together, and watch Match of the Day in
it the same night.'

The basic assumption was that most of the Habitat stock – wood,
plastic, ethnic basket-work, chromium plate and giant floor-cushions
– would somehow mix and match in all its possible combinations to
make an acceptable background for a modern middle-class way of
life.

Pop Art, the form of visual expression for which the 1960s will be
best remembered, naturally had an impact on the typical interior of
the time. But its influence made itself felt more in soft furnishings,
decorative objects and knick-knacks than it did in actual furniture.
Few homes could afford the sado-masochistic girl-table designed by
the Pop painter Allen Jones, and it is extremely improbable that one-
off furniture of this type was ever made to serve any practical purpose.
Pop music, on the other hand, did have a very definite impact. The
most obvious thing it did was to promote the sale of elaborate hi-fi

188

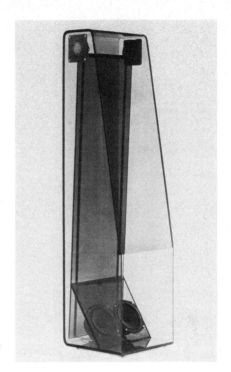

183 Technological emphasis. Acrylic
loudspeaker by Quadrant 4

equipment. The prestige of the music somehow rubbed off on the 183
equipment needed to reproduce it, and the loudspeakers and other
necessary components were given undisguised prominence in many a
living-room. Rock in its psychedelic phase in the late 1960s spawned
not only posters but patterns for fabrics; and the philosophy of tune
in, turn on and drop out probably had something to do with the
popularity of the water-bed, which became one of the erotic status
symbols of the period. 'Ethnic' furniture – basket-work chairs and
other items imported from the Third World – owed something to
sheer economics (they were usually very cheap, just as East Indian
goods had been in the seventeenth century), and something to the
new fashion for the crafts, but perhaps most of all to Pop music's
promotion of a concern for ecology and the environment, and the
cult of supposedly natural things which made the fortune of many a
health-food shop. Pop Art was thus confronted with a kind of anti-
Pop which nevertheless had the same roots as itself.

It is not certain that the Deco revival should actually be classified
under the heading of Modernism at all, as in the strict sense it was

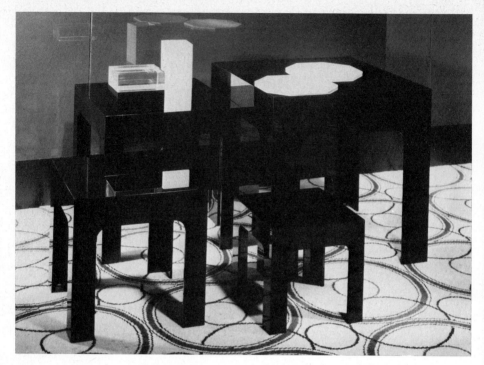

184 Deco Revival. Acrylic nesting tables designed by Albrizzi Ltd, 1970s

simply a fresh manifestation of the eclectic revivalism which had been going on since the mid eighteenth century. Prices for genuine Deco objects soared; by the late 1970s good examples of furniture by Coard 148 and Ruhlmann had outstripped all but their most expensive eighteenth-century rivals. At the same time a new brand of Deco-inspired furniture began to make its appearance, something which, interestingly enough, did not happen when there was an equivalent and rather earlier collectors' craze for Art Nouveau. These Retro pieces, as I shall call them to distinguish them from genuine Art Deco, were sometimes the work of fashionable decorators, who produced 166, 184 designs in steel, glass, brass and lacquer (or plastic imitating lacquer) which owed more perhaps to Deco architectural details than to specific originals by leading 1920s designers. Sometimes, too, there was a Deco touch to the furniture produced by firms catering to the upper end of the mass-market. These designs often inclined towards the use of metal and glass, and could be seen as challengers to the

202

185 (*opposite*) Visual muzak. Foyer of the Park Tower Hotel, London, designed by Richard Seifert and Partners, 1973

somewhat more expensive Classic Modern items which competed for the same sector of the furniture-market.

Finally, there is the style I have labelled Post Modern, following a system of categorization recently proposed by certain architectural historians. It may be thought that the territory assigned to Post Modern can be divided on the one hand between that assigned to Package Modern, with its relaxed and pragmatic attitude towards modern design in general; and that given to Retro, which deliberately challenges the logic and purity of Classic Modernism while for the most part using typically modern materials. On the other hand, there is a need to find a way of describing and perhaps defining an elusive kind of environment which most of us know and few of us bother to think about. This environment is as protean and as difficult to seize intellectually as muzak. Like muzak, it is to be found chiefly in public *185* places – in airport lounges, shops and the foyers of luxury hotels. It reaches its apogee in the gambling casinos of Las Vegas. If the Post Modern style has a parent, it is Morris Lapidus, who was responsible for styling a whole series of resort hotels in Florida during the 1950s. It has been said of Lapidus that 'he mixes all the popular periods of interior design – Louis XIV, Robert Adam, Moderne Streamlined – in a distinctive but unclassifiable style.' Part of its unclassifiability is due to the unabashed combination of eclectic decoration and modern services, such as air-conditioning and concealed lighting; and modern materials, particularly all forms of synthetics and plastics. A whole series of such interiors were created in London during the hotel-building boom between 1969 and 1974. Post Modernism relies for its effect, not on any single item in a decor, but on an often incongruous mixture of items. The surrealist influence which made itself felt in some aspects of popular design in the post-war period thus continues an underground existence in Post Modern decor.

It makes itself occasionally visible elsewhere, in the fantasy furniture which has cropped up occasionally during the post-war *188* epoch. This has taken a number of very different guises – Jones's girl-table has already been mentioned, and has definite surrealist as well as Pop overtones. To this can be added some designs by the Italian, Fornasetti, often making use of plastic laminates. More strictly surrealist still is furniture by François Xavier Lalanne – a secretaire in the form of a rhinoceros, stools made to look like a flock of sheep. In the United States, biomorphic forms closely related to this more

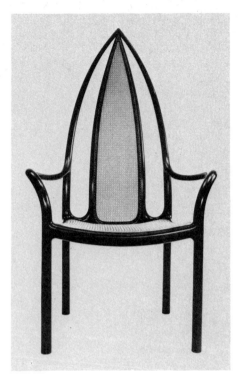

186 Sycamore and walnut dining-chair by Williamson

187 Ebony and nickel-silver chair designed by Makepeace, and made in his workshop in 1978

188 Allen Jones, *Table Sculpture*. Painted glass fibre and resin, with tailor-made accessories, 1969

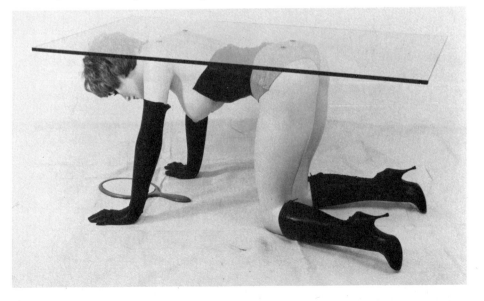

abstract aspect of surrealism have been used by the leading artist-
189 craftsman Wendell Castle.

Castle's furniture is even more interesting looked at from a different point of view. It is defiantly hand-made, carved into intricate forms which no machine could be asked to produce. Castle himself is a leading figure in a craft revival which has also made itself felt in England, with craftsmen such as John Makepeace, Rupert
186 Williamson, Richard La Trobe Bateman and Martin Grierson. Makepeace is the senior figure in this group. Unlike Castle, he sometimes undertakes contract work, and does not work upon every piece of furniture himself. Rather, he will turn a particular design over to one member of his workshop, who is thenceforth responsible for its embodiment. But the most typical part of his production is similar to Castle's in one respect: it is emphatically something which the machine cannot hope to rival. A chair recently produced in the
187 Makepeace workshops consists of more than 2,000 pieces of ebony. These are used to produce a sinuous Gothic form which triumphs over the stubborn and intractable nature of the material. This chair, in fact, is a deliberate *tour de force*, a demonstration of supreme mastery of technique. As such, it flouts the rules solemnly laid down by the original founders of the Arts and Crafts Movement in the nineteenth century, and must be linked instead to the work of a Riesener or a Roentgen in the eighteenth. It aims to remove some furniture at least from the industrial category and put it on a level with the work of the 'fine' artist. In terms of the degree of skill required, it presents a far more demanding challenge than most contemporary artists ever have to face.

Indeed, one of the reasons why craftwork has experienced such a revival in the 1960s and 1970s seems to be impatience with the way the 'fine' arts are going, and a hunger for a display of skill which painters and sculptors are no longer willing to provide. Makepeace's chair, which shows both Gothic and Art Nouveau influences in its design, has one characteristic which makes it seem peculiarly modern. It demands to be looked at more or less in isolation. If it is added to an interior, it takes its place as a piece of sculpture would. People do not find this strange because the decorators, and after them the surrealists, have accustomed us to think of an interior as being essentially a collage, an artistic statement made up of other statements which are to some extent in conflict with one another.

This tendency seems at least as strong as the contrary impulse which also asserts itself powerfully in our own day – towards the completely integrated capsule for living, where furniture and interior architecture will be indistinguishable from one another.

Furniture responds to many impulses, practical and aesthetic. In the late eighteenth century chairs grew narrower when it was no longer necessary to accommodate the width of hooped skirts. After the Second World War, the room-divider made its appearance, both as a concession to the desire for a freer flow of interior space; and as an admission that living-areas would now have to be used more economically, to satisfy several functions at once. But the expressive function is at least as important as any other; and has tended to become more important as more attention is concentrated on the personality of the individual. Logic demands the complete standardization and industrialization of all furniture production; psychology indicates that this will never happen. The contradictory nature of the human animal appears as plainly in this field as it does in most of the other spheres of his activity.

189 Laminated cherrywood settee designed by Castle, 1968

Bibliography

ADAMS, LOUIS, *Décorations intérieures et meubles des époques Louis XIII et Louis XIV*, Paris 1865

AGIUS, PAULINE, 'Late Sixteenth and Seventeenth Century Furniture in Oxford', *Furniture History* (Leeds 1971)

ALISON, FILIPPO, *Charles Rennie Mackintosh as a Designer of Chairs*, London 1971, Woodbury 1978

AMAYA, MARIO, *Art Nouveau*, London, New York 1966

ASLIN, ELIZABETH, *19th Century English Furniture*, London, Salem 1962

BACCHESCHI, EDI, *Mobili genovesi*, Milan 1962

—, *Mobili italiani del rinascimento*, Milan 1962

BAKER, HOLLIS S., *Furniture in the Ancient World*, London, New York 1966

BALDWIN, BILLY, *Billy Baldwin Decorates*, New York, Chicago and San Francisco 1972

BATTERSBY, MARTIN, *The Decorative Twenties*, London, New York 1969

—, *The Decorative Thirties*, London 1970, New York 1971

BAYER, HERBERT, (ED.), WALTER GROPIUS AND ISE GROPIUS, *Bauhaus 1919–1928*, Boston 1959, London 1976

BEER, EILEENE HARRISON, *Scandinavian Design: Objects of a Lifestyle*, New York 1975

BERLAGE, HENDRIK PETRUS, *Over stijl in bouw- en meubelkunst*, Rotterdam 1908

BLAKE, PETER, *Le Corbusier: Architecture and Form*, London 1960, Baltimore 1964

BONNAFFÉ, EDMOND, 'Le meuble en France au XVIe siècle', *Gazette des Beaux-Arts*, XXXII–XXXV (Paris 1885–87)

BOYNTON, LINDSAY, 'The Hardwick Hall Inventory of 1601', *Furniture History* (Leeds 1971)

BRUNHAMMER, YVONNE, *Meubles et ensembles Restauration/Louis-Philippe*, Paris n.d.

—, and Monique de Fayet, *Meubles et ensembles: époques Louis XIII et Louis XIV*, Paris 1966

BURR, GRACE HARDENDORFF, *Hispanic Furniture* (2nd edn), New York 1964

Centre National d'Art et de Culture Georges Pompidou, Paris, 'Paris-Berlin, 1900–1933' (exh. cat.), Paris 1978

CHIESA, G., *Il quattrocento: mobili, arti decorative, costume*, Milan 1971

—, *Il cinquecento: mobili, arti decorative, costume*, Milan 1972

—, *Il seicento: mobili, arti decorative, costume*, Milan 1973

CITO FILOMARINO, ANNA-MARIA, *L'ottocento: i mobili del tempo dei nonni*, Milan 1969

CLARK, ROBERT JUDSON (ed.), *The Arts and Crafts Movement in America, 1876–1916*, Princeton 1972

COLERIDGE, ANTHONY, *Chippendale Furniture*, London, New York 1968

COLOMBO, SILVANO, *L'arte del mobile in Italia*, Milan 1975

CORNFORTH, JOHN, *English Interiors, 1790–1848*, London 1978

Council of Europe, 'The Age of Neo-Classicism' (exh. cat.), London 1972

—, 'Tendenzen der zwanziger Jahre' (exh. cat.), Berlin 1977

DE BELLAIGUE, GEOFFREY, and PATRICIA KIRKHAM, 'George IV and the Furnishing of Windsor Castle', *Furniture History* (Leeds 1971)

DE FUSCO, RENATO, *Le Corbusier Designer–Furniture, 1929*, Milan 1976, Woodbury 1977

DE WOLFE, ELSIE, *After All: From Colonial Times to the 20th Century*, London 1935, New York 1974

Design in the Festival, London 1951

Die Durchgeistigung der deutschen Arbeit: Jahrbuch des deutschen Werkbundes, Jena 1912

EAMES, PENELOPE, *Medieval Furniture*, London 1977

EDWARDS, RALPH, and MARGARET JOURDAIN, *Georgian Cabinet-Makers*, (rev. edn.), London 1955

ERIKSEN, SVEND, *Early Neo-Classicism in France*, London, Salem 1974

EUDES, GEORGES, *Modern French Interiors*, London 1958, New York 1959

FANIEL, STÉPHANE (ed.), *Le dix-septième siècle français*, Paris 1958

FAYET, MONIQUE DE, *Meubles et ensembles moyen âge et renaissance*, Paris 1961

FEDUCHI, L., *El mueble español*, Barcelona 1969

Fine Art Society Ltd, 'The Arts and Crafts Movement' (exh. cat.), London 1973

FISCHER, ERNST, *Svenska möbler i bild*, Stockholm 1950

Fischer Fine Art, 'Josef Hoffmann' (exh. cat.), London 1977

FISHER, RICHARD B., *Syrie Maugham*, London 1978

FORMAN, BENNO M., 'Continental Furniture Craftsmen in London: 1511–1625', *Furniture History* (Leeds 1971)

FOWLER, JOHN, and JOHN CORNFORTH, *English Decoration in the 18th Century*, London 1974

FREY, GILBERT, *The Modern Chair: 1850 to Today*, London, New York 1970

Gemeentemuseum, The Hague, 'Meubelen/Furniture 1600–1800', (exh. cat.), The Hague 1975

GILBERN, CRAIG, *The Reliance on Tradition, 1625–1700*, Columbus (Ohio) 1969

GILLIATT, MARY, *English Style*, London, New York 1967

GLOAG, JOHN, *The Englishman's Chair*, London 1964

—, *A Social History of Furniture Design*, London, New York 1966

GOLFIERI, ENNIO, *La casa faentina dell'ottocento*, 2 vols, Faenza 1970

GRANDJEAN, SERGE, *Empire Furniture 1800–1825*, London, Salem 1966

HARLING, ROBERT (ed.), *The Modern Interior*, London 1964, New York 1965

—, *House & Garden's Guide to Interior Decoration*, London, Toronto 1967

HARRIS, EILEEN, *Furniture of Robert Adam*, London 1963

HATJE, GERD, and PETER KASPER, *Design for Modern Living*, London 1975, published in the USA as *Decorating Ideas for Modern Living*, New York 1977

HAYWARD, HELENA (ed.), *World Furniture*, London, New York 1965

HEAL, AMBROSE, *The London Furniture Makers*, London 1953, New York 1972

HEWITT, LINDA, *Chippendale and All the Rest*, South Brunswick (New York), London 1949

HICKS, DAVID, *On Decoration*, London 1966, New York 1967

HILLIER, BEVIS, *Art Deco of the Twenties and Thirties*, London, New York 1968

—, *Austerity/Binge: The Decorative Arts of the Forties and Fifties*, London, New York 1975

HIMMELHEBER, GEORG, *Biedermeier Furniture*, London, Salem 1974
JANNEAU, GUILLAUME, *Le meuble léger en France*, Paris 1952
JENCKS, CHARLES, *The Language of Post-Modern Architecture* (rev. edn), New York 1977, London 1978
JERVIS, SIMON, *Printed Furniture Designs before 1650*, London 1974
—, *High Victorian Design*, Ottawa 1974
JOEL, DAVID, *Furniture Design Set Free* (rev. edn), London 1969
JOHNSON, STEWARD, *Eileen Gray: Designer 1879–1976*, London 1979
JOURDAIN, MARGARET, *English Decoration and Furniture of the Early Renaissance (1500–1650)*, London, New York 1924
—, *Regency Furniture 1795–1820* (2nd edn), London, New York 1948
—, *The Work of William Kent*, London, New York 1948
—, *English Interior Decoration, 1500–1830*, London, New York 1950
—, *Stuart Furniture at Knole*, London 1952
—, and F. Rose, *English Furniture: The Georgian Period (1750–1830)*, London 1953
JOY, EDWARD T., 'Some Aspects of the London Furniture Industry in the 18th Century' (unpublished Ph.D. thesis), 1966
—, *English Furniture 1800–1851*, London 1977
KENWORTHY-BROWNE, JOHN, *Chippendale and His Contemporaries*, London, New York 1973
KREISEL, HEINRICH, *Die Kunst des deutschen Möbels*, Munich 1968–73
KRON, JOAN and SUZANNE SLEZIN, *Hi-Tech*, New York 1978
KRÜGER, FRITZ, *El mobiliario popular en los paises románicos*, Coimbra 1963
LANCASTER, OSBERT, *Here, of All Places* (incl. *Homes, Sweet Homes* and *Pillar to Post*), London 1959
LESIEUTRE, ALAIN *The Spirit and Splendour of Art Deco*, London, New York 1974
LÉVY-COBLENTZ, FRANÇOISE, *L'art du meuble en Alsace*, vol. 1, Strasbourg 1975
LIVERSIDGE, JOAN, *Furniture in Roman Britain*, London 1955
MARGON, LESTER, *Masterpieces of American Furniture, 1620–1840*, New York 1965
MATTHEAU, JACQUES (ed.), *Meubles et ensembles Directoire/Empire*, Paris n.d.
MAZZARIOL, GIUSEPPE, *Mobili italiani del seicento e del settecento*, Milan 1963
Metropolitan Museum of Art, New York, '19th Century America: Furniture and other Decorative Arts' (exh. cat.), New York 1970
—, 'The Art of Joinery' (exh. cat.), New York 1972
MEUVRET, JEAN, *Les ébénistes du XVIIIe siècle français*, Paris 1963
MOLINIER, EMILE, *Histoire générale des arts appliqués à l'industrie*, vol. 2 ('Les meubles du moyen âge et de la renaissance'), Paris 1905
MORAZZONI, GIUSEPPE, *Mobili veneziani laccati*, Milan 1958
MUSGRAVE, CLIFFORD, *Regency Furniture, 1800–1830*, London 1961, (2nd edn) Salem 1970
NAYLOR, GILLIAN, *The Arts and Crafts Movement*, London, Cambridge (Mass.) 1971
NORBURY, JAMES, *The World of Victoriana*, London 1972
ODOM, WILLIAM, *Italian Renaissance Furniture* (2nd edn), New York 1966–67
OVERY, PAUL, *De Stijl*, London 1969
PACKER, CHARLES, *Paris Furniture by the Master Ebénistes*, Newport (Mon.) 1956

PEVSNER, NIKOLAUS, *The Sources of Modern Architecture and Design*, London 1968, New York 1977
PHILIPPE, JOSEPH, *Le mobilier liégeois*, Liège 1962
QUIMBY, IAN M.G. (ed.), *Arts of the American Community in the Seventeenth Century* (Winterthur Conference Report, 1974), Charlottesville 1975
REEVES, DAVID L., *Furniture: an Explanatory History* (rev. edn), London 1959
RICHTER, GISELA M.A., *The Furniture of the Greeks, Etruscans and Romans* (new edn), London 1966
RITTER, ENRICHETTA, *Design Italiano: Mobili*, Milan/Rome 1969
Royal Academy of Arts, London, '50 Years: Bauhaus' (exh. cat.), London 1966
—, 'Victorian and Edwardian Decorative Art: the Handley-Read Collection' (exh. cat.), London 1972
SCHAEFER, HERWIN, *The Roots of Modern Design: the Functional Tradition in the Nineteenth Century*, London 1970
SCHMUTZLER, ROBERT, *Art Nouveau*, New York 1962, London 1964
SCHOFIELD, MARIA (ed.), *Decorative Art and Modern Interiors, 1978*, London, New York 1978
SHEA, JOHN G., *The American Shakers and their Furniture*, New York 1971, Wokingham 1972
Stile degli anni '70: i mobili, Lo, Milan 1970
STILLMAN, DAMIE, *The Decorative Work of Robert Adam*, London, Levittown 1966
SYMONDS, ROBERT WEMYSS, *English Furniture from Charles II to George II*, London 1929
—, *Furniture Making in Seventeenth and Eighteenth Century England*, London 1955
—, and B.B. Whineray, *Victorian Furniture*, London 1962
THORNTON, PETER, 'A Short Commentary on the Hardwick Inventory of 1601', *Furniture History* (Leeds 1971)
Trinity College, Dublin, *Chairs, 1918–1970* (exh. cat.), Dublin 1971
VERLET, PIERRE, *Le mobilier royal français*, Paris 1945
—, *Le mobilier royal français*, vol. 2, Paris 1955
—, *French Royal Furniture*, (trs. from the French by M. Bullock), London, New York 1963
—, *The Eighteenth Century in France*, Rutland (Vermont), Tokyo and London 1967
— (ed.), *Styles, meubles, décors, du moyen âge à nos jours*, 2 vols, Paris 1972
Victoria & Albert Museum, London, 'Osterley Park' (exh. cat.), London 1972
—, 'The American Museum of Art and Design: Designs from the Cooper-Hewitt Museum, New York' (exh. cat.), London 1973
—, 'The Way We Live Now: Designs for Interiors 1950 to the Present Day' (exh. cat.), London 1978
VINCENT, CLARE, 'John Henry Belter's Patent Parlour Furniture', *Furniture History* (Leeds 1974)
WARD-JACKSON, PETER, *English Furniture Designs of the 18th Century*, London 1958
WATSON, FRANK JOHN BAGOLT, *The Wrightsman Collection*, vols 1, 2, New York 1966
WINDISCH-GRAETZ, F., *Le meuble baroque et rococo*, Paris 1959
WITZEMANN, HERTA-MARIA, *Deutsche Möbel heute*, Stuttgart 1954
WOLSEY, SAMUEL WILFRED, and R.W.P. LUFF, *Furniture in England: The Age of the Joiner*, London 1968, New York 1969

List of illustrations

Dimensions are given in inches and centimetres: height, width and depth

49 *Cassapanca.* 33 × 98 × 29 (83·8 × 249 × 73·7). Victoria and Albert Museum, London.

50 *Cassone.* Late 16th century. Copyright the Frick Collection, New York.

51 Inlaid table. Victoria and Albert Museum, London.

52 Venetian folding chair. H. 41, w. 27½ (104 × 69·9). Victoria and Albert Museum, London.

53 Walnut cabinet. Late 16th century. 63 × 69⅝ × 21¼ (160 × 176·5 × 56). Copyright the Frick Collection, New York.

54 Spanish folding armchair. Metropolitan Museum of Art, New York, gift of George Blumenthal, 1941.

55 *Vargueño.* Walnut. 54⅓ × 37¾ × 17½ (138 × 96 × 44·5). Courtesy of the Hispanic Society of America.

56 Oak armchair. 48 × 24 × 15 (121·9 × 61 × 38). Victoria and Albert Museum, London.

57 Marble-topped tables from the Lumley Inventory. Collection of the Earl of Scarbrough. Photo Gerald Sunderland.

58 Banquet at the court of Emperor Rudolph II in Prague. German. Osterreichische Nationalbibliothek, Vienna, MS. Cod. 7906 f. 16v–17.

59 North Drawing-room, Ham House. Photo Victoria and Albert Museum, London. Crown copyright.

60 Vermeer (1632–75), *The Music Lesson.* Oil on canvas, 29 × 25¼ (73·6 × 64·1). Reproduced by gracious permission of Her Majesty Queen Elizabeth II.

61 Early Stuart upholstered settee. Photo National Trust.

62 Oriental lacquer cabinet on English stand. 62¾ × 54 × 26 (159·4 × 137·2 × 66). Victoria and Albert Museum, London.

63 Walnut armchair. 54½ × 28½ × 22½ (138·4 × 72·4 × 57·2). Victoria and Albert Museum, London.

64 Veneered oak cabinet. Reproduced by permission of the Trustees, the Wallace Collection, London.

65 Silver furniture from the King's Bedroom, Knole, Kent. Photo National Trust.

66 Wooden cabinet made for John Evelyn. Victoria and Albert Museum, London.

67 The Galerie des Glaces (1678–84) by Jules-Hardouin Mansart and Charles le Brun, Versailles. Photo John Webb.

68 Louis XIV visiting the Gobelins manufactory. French. Gobelins Museum, Paris. Photo Giraudon.

69 The *Lotterie Royale.* Anonymous engraving. Bibliothèque Nationale, Paris.

70 Doll's house made for the Stromer family of Nuremberg. Germanisches National Museum, Nuremberg.

71 Bookcases from Pepys' library, Buckingham Street, London. Now in the Pepys Library, Cambridge. Photo courtesy of the Master and Fellows of Magdalene College, Cambridge.

72 Walnut writing-table, with movable case of drawers, and seaweed marquetry. Now in Windsor Castle. Reproduced by gracious permission of Her Majesty Queen Elizabeth II.

73 Bosse, *Winter.* From a set of engravings of the seasons. Bibliothèque Nationale, Paris. Photo Giraudon.

74 Armchair designed by Brustolon. Italy, 1700. H. 49½ (125·7). Museo di Ca' Rezzonico, Venice.

75 Steen (1625–79), *The Prince's Birthday*, *c.* 1660. Oil on oak, 18⅛ × 24⅝ (46 × 62·5). Rijksmuseum, Amsterdam.

76 Crespi (*c.* 1598–1630), *St Charles Borromeo Fasting*, *c.* 1628. Oil on canvas. Chiesa della Passione, Milan. Photo Alinari.

77 Van Blarenberghe, miniature on a snuff box by A. Leferre, *c.* 1771. 3⅛ × 2⅜ × 1½ (8·9 × 6 × 3·8). Louvre, Paris. Photo Bulloz

78 De Troy (1645–1730), *A Reading from Molière*, *c.* 1710. Oil on canvas, 29 × 35½ (73·6 × 90·1). Private Collection. Photo Giraudon.

79 Hussey (1713–83), *Interior with Members of the Corbally Family.* Oil on canvas, 24½ × 30 (62 × 72). National Gallery of Ireland, Dublin. Photo Richard Green (Fine Paintings) Ltd, London.

80 Drawing by the Frères Slodtz for the commode in *81*. Cabinet des Estampes, Bibliothèque Nationale, Paris.

81 Commode with serpentine marble top. Veneered on oak with kingwood and mahogany. 35 × 77 × 31¾ (88·9 × 195·6 × 80·6). Reproduced by permission of the Trustees, the Wallace Collection, London.

82 Cabinet by Weisweiler (active *c.* 1778–1809). Oak veneered with thuya, satin and purple woods. 47¾ × 30 × 14 (121·3 × 76·2 × 35·6). Reproduced by permission of the Trustees, the Wallace Collection, London.

83 Louis XV lacquer commode, signed B.V.R.B. (working before 1736–*c.* 1765). 34½ × 63½ × 25 (87·6 × 161·3 × 63·5). Photo courtesy of Partridge (Fine Arts) Ltd, London.

84 The Reichen Zimmer (1730–37), the Residenz, Munich. Photo Bildarchiv Foto Marburg.

85 Painted and decorated secretaire-cabinet in the baroque style. Photo courtesy of Sotheby Parke Bernet & Co., New York.

86 Marquetry *coiffeuse.* 32½ × 39¼ × 24 (82 × 100 × 61). Photo courtesy of Sotheby Parke Bernet & Co., London.

87 A pair of giltwood stands. 50 × 10⅜ × 12⅜ (127 × 27·3 × 32·4). Victoria and Albert Museum, London.

88 Sheraton, design for a drawing-room chair. From *The Cabinet-Maker and Upholsterer's Drawing Book*, 1793–94.

89 Commode attributed to Langlois. 34 × 52½ × 23½ (86·4 × 133·4 × 59·7). Victoria and Albert Museum, London.

90 Gothic-backed Windsor chair. 36½ × 23½ × 24 (91·4 × 59·7 × 61). Victoria and Albert Museum, London.

91 Chippendale-style side-chair. Cuban or Honduras mahogany with strapwork splat back. Seat covered in green damask. 39 × 26½ × 22¼ (99 × 67·3 × 56·5). Metropolitan Museum of Art, New York, Collection of Irwin Untermyer.

92 Bedstead in chinese taste. Probably made by Chippendale after a design in *The Director*, 1754. 150 × 95 × 102 (381 × 241·3 × 259). Victoria and Albert Museum, London.

93 *The Music Room*, Royal Pavilion, Brighton, 1822, from Nash, *Views of the Royal Pavilion*, 1826.

94 The Holbein Chamber, Strawberry Hill, Photo Country Life.

95 Adam, designs for dining-room furniture for Osterley Park.

96 The Harewood Desk. Mahogany and oak, veneered with formal designs in rosewood, satinwood and other stained woods, with ormolu mounts. 33½ × 81 × 47½ (85 × 205·7 × 120·6). Collection of the Leeds City Art Galleries (Temple Newsam House).

97 Weisweiler side-table with *pietre dure* panels. Reproduced by gracious permission of Her Majesty Queen Elizabeth II.

98 Carved and giltwood armchair made for the Comte d'Artois. 1777. Louvre, Paris. Photo Documentation Photographique de la Réunion des Musées Nationaux, Paris.

99 Day-bed. Beechwood lacquered in gold and silver on scarlet. Made by Grendey (*c.* 1693–1780) for export to Spain. English, *c.* 1730. 39 × 76 × 31½ (99 × 193 × 80). Victoria and Albert Museum, London.

100 American block-front bureau. Boston. *c.* 1770. 44½ × 42 (113 × 106). Reproduced by permission of the American Museum in Britain, Bath.

101 David (1748–1825), *The Loves of Paris and Helen.* Oil on canvas, 57·5 × 167·3 (146 × 425). Louvre, Paris. Photo Giraudon.

102 Davis, study for a Greek Revival double parlour, *c.* 1830. Photo courtesy of The New-York Historical Society, New York City.

103 'Egyptian' chair designed by Hope. Buscot Park, Berkshire. Photo National Trust.

104 The 'Egyptian' Room, from Hope, *Household Furniture and Interior Decoration*, 1807.

105 French bed and wardrobe, from Smith, *A Collection of Designs for Household Furniture and Interior Decoration*, 1808.

106 Paris bedroom of Monsieur O, from Percier and Fontaine, *Recueil de Décorations Intérieures*, 1801.

107 Garneray, *The Music Room at Malmaison.* Château de Malmaison. Photo Giraudon.

108 Mahogany side-chair. Part of a set with armchairs made by Phyfe for William Bayard of New York City in 1807. 33 × 19 × 21⅛

(83·8 × 48·2 × 53·7). Courtesy of the Henry Francis du Pont Winterthur Museum, Winterthur.
109 Walnut chair. Museen für Kunst und Kulturgeschichte der Hansestadt, Lubeck.
110 *Chaise à l'officier*. Mahogany and gilded bronze. Musée des Arts Décoratifs, Paris. Photo Giraudon.
111 Mechanical desk. Mahogany and gilded bronze. Château de Malmaison. Photo Archives Photographiques, Paris.
112 'Egyptian' river-boat couch with crocodile feet. Green painted wood with carved and gilt enrichments of dolphins, scallop shells, serpents and reeds. Royal Pavilion, Art Gallery and Museums, Brighton.
113 Furniture from the Trafalgar Suite. London, 1813. Royal Pavilion, Art Gallery and Museums, Brighton. Photo Radio Times Hulton Picture Library.
114 The drawing-room at Eaton Hall, from J.C. Buckler *Views of Eaton Hall*, 1826.
115 Chair designed by Pugin and probably made by the firm of J.G. Crace. Victoria and Albert Museum, London.
116 The library, Scotney Castle, Kent. Photo Country Life.
117 Circular upholstered sofa, *c.* 1850. Victoria and Albert Museum, London.
118 Brass four-poster bed, from M.D. Wyatt *Industrial Arts of the Nineteenth Century*, 1851.
119 Metal and upholstered rocking chair. English.
120 Papier-mâché settee. English, *c.* 1850. 43 × 69½ × 25 (109·2 × 176·5 × 63·5). Victoria and Albert Museum, London.
121 Thonet bentwood chair. Victoria and Albert Museum, London.
122 Side-chair by Belter. H. 41 (104·1). Wadsworth Atheneum, Hartford, gift of Mrs Stephen B. Stanton.
123 Mahogany cabinet. Cross-banded in kingwood and inlaid with brass and ebony borders. Photo courtesy of Sotheby Parke Bernet & Co., London.
124 Shaker tilt-leg chair. Maplewood with cane seat. Made at Harvard, *c.* 1850. 38 × 17 × 13 (96·5 × 43·2 × 33). Fruitlands Museums, Harvard, Mass.
125 American Windsor settee. Wood painted black. *c.* 1800. Metropolitan Museum of Art, New York, gift of Mr and Mrs Paul Moore, 1946.
126 Headboard designed by Burges. Mahogany painted red, carved, stencilled and gilded; painting by Holiday, *The Sleeping Beauty*, 1867. Photo courtesy of the Trustees of the Cecil Higgins Art Gallery, Bedford.
127 Giraud, *The Library of the Princesse Mathilde at her Country House, Saint-Gratien*. Collection Pierre Fabius, Paris.
128 De Fournier, *Cabinet de Travail, Château de Compiègne*. Château de Compiègne. Photo Giraudon.
129 Treffy Dunn (*fl.* 1870–90), *Rossetti in his Sitting-room*, 1882. 21¼ × 32¼ (54 × 81·9). National Portrait Gallery, London.
130 The Green Room, designed by Webb for the South Kensington Museum. Made by Morris & Co. Victoria and Albert Museum, London.
131 Stained wood chair with rush seat. 35 × 19½ × 18½ (88·9 × 49·5 × 47). Victoria and Albert Museum, London.
132 Rush-seated and turned chair designed by Madox Brown. Photo courtesy of the Arts Council of Great Britain.
133 Library bookcase. From Eastlake, *Hints on Household Taste*, 1868.
134 Satinwood cabinet with brass mountings, ivory handles and painted panels representing the four seasons. 70 × 50½ × 16 (177·8 × 128·3 × 40·6). Ebonized oak chair with upholstered seat and back and turned decoration on the legs. 42 × 24 (106·6 × 61). Both manufactured by William Watt. Victoria and Albert Museum, London.
135 Chair designed by Mackmurdo. William Morris Gallery, Walthamstow.
136 Grimshaw (1836–93), *Summer: The Artist's Wife in the Morning Room of their Home, Knostrop Old Hall, near Leeds*, 1875. 25 × 30 (63 × 76). Photo courtesy of Roy Miles Fine Painting.
137 Interior of Grimson's cottage, Sapperton. Photo Leicestershire Museums, Art Galleries and Records Service.
138 Chair designed by Hoffmann. H. 28¾ (73). Photo courtesy of Fischer Fine Art, London.
139 Armchair designed by Wright. Wood. 32 × 23 × 23 (81·3 × 58·4 × 58·4). Albright-Knox Art Gallery, Buffalo, New York, gift of Darwin R. Martin.
140 Oak and leather library table manufactured by Stickley, *c.* 1906. H. 30 (76·2). Metropolitan Museum of Art, New York, gift of Cyril Farny in memory of Phyllis Holt, 1976.
141 The main bedroom, The Hill House, Hellensburgh. Photograph taken in 1904. Photo National Monuments Record.
142 Tiffany (1848–1933), spider-web table-lamp with leaded glass shade on a bronze and mosaic glass base designed as a flowering narcissus. Photo courtesy of Christie, Manson & Woods International, Inc.
143 The 'Nénuphar' writing-table. Mahogany with gilt bronze mounts. 41⅓ × 70½ × 40½ (105 × 179 × 103). Musée de l'Ecole de Nancy.
144 Bedroom designed by Benn, from Shapland, *Style Schemes in Antique Furnishings*, 1909.
145 Armchair designed by Van der Velde. 1898–99. 34¼ × 27 (98·7 × 68·5). Nordenfjeldske Kunstindustrimuseum, Trondheim.
146 Bedroom designed by Martine, Paris. *c.* 1924. From *Art et Décoration*, 1924.
147 Drawing-room designed by Ruhlmann. Photo courtesy of Philippe Garner.
148 Cabinet designed by Ruhlmann. Photo courtesy of Philippe Garner.
149 Stool made by Legrain for Doucet. Photo courtesy of Philippe Garner.
150 *Le Salon de Verre*, designed by Gray. From *L'Illustration*, 1933. Photo courtesy of Philippe Garner.
151 Pye Twin Triple portable battery radio, 1930. From Jonathan Hill, *The Cat's Whisker*, 1978. Photo courtesy of Oresko Books Ltd.
152 Corner of the *Grand Salon* of the liner *Normandie*. From *Art et Décoration*, 1935.
153 Sideboard designed by Rietveld. 41 × 78¼ × 17¾ (104 × 200 × 45). Stedelijk Museum, Amsterdam.
154 Wassily chair by Breuer. 1969 replica of the original 1925 chair. University of East Anglia Collection, Norwich.
155 Cantilever chair by Mies van der Rohe. 29½ × 22 × 35 (75 × 55·9 × 88·9). Victoria and Albert Museum, London.
156 Dining-table and chair made from tubular steel by Pel Ltd. Victoria and Albert Museum, London. Photo courtesy of Pel Ltd.
157 'Le grand confort' chair. Tubular steel with Havana leather cushions. French. 23⅝ × 17¾ × 31½ (60 × 45 × 80). Musée des Arts Décoratifs, Paris.
158 Armchair 406. Webbing seat. Photo courtesy of Artek, Finland.
159 Set of stacking chairs by Alvar Aalto. Photo Royal Academy of Arts, London.
160 Patent drawing of Dymaxion bathroom. Photo courtesy of Buckminster Fuller Archives.
161 Kitchen furniture. From Heal & Son Ltd, 151st catalogue. Photo courtesy Heal and Son Ltd, London.
162 An interior view of Queen Mary's doll's house. Reproduced by gracious permission of Her Majesty Queen Elizabeth II.
163 Fall-front writing-cabinet. Photo courtesy Gordon Russell Ltd, Worcestershire.
164 Syrie Maugham's drawing-room. From *The Studio*, 1933.
165 Marlene Dietrich's private sitting-room which she designed and furnished herself. Early 1930s. Photo the Cinema Book Shop, London.
166 Ziggurat dining-table. Early 1970s. H. 29, d. 60 (H. 73, d. 152). Photo Mann Brothers, London.
167 Utility dressing-table. Photo courtesy of Sir Gordon Russell.

168 DAR chair, manufactured by Herman Miller Ltd. 1948. 31½ × 25⅝ × 24¾ (80 × 65 × 62). Photo Herman Miller Ltd, London.
169 Tulip chair. Moulded fibreglass shell on aluminium pedestal. North American. 32 × 26 × 23½ (81·3 × 66 × 59·7). Victoria and Albert Museum, London.
170 Stainless steel and canework chair. Danish. L. 62, W. 26 (L. 157·5, W. 66). Victoria and Albert Museum, London.
171 Antelope chair. English, 1951. Photo Race Ltd, a member of the Alcocks Laird Group.
172 Swan chair. Leather and aluminium swivel chair on four-branched foot. Danish. 30 × 29½ × 26 (76 × 75 × 66). Victoria and Albert Museum, London.
173 Three stool-chairs designed by Bertoia.
174 Mae West Hot Lips Sofa. Upholstered in shocking pink. 33⅞ × 71¼ × 31½ (86 × 182 × 80). Edward James Foundation, Sussex.
175 Ami 'A' juke box. 1946–48. H. 66½ (169). Reproduced by kind permission of Sotheby's, Belgravia.
176 Sketch for dining-room. Pencil, crayon, water and body colour. c. 1973. Photo Aram Designs Ltd.
177 Blow chair. Photo courtesy of Zanotta of Milan.
178 Sacco chair. Photo courtesy of Zanotta of Milan.

179 Le Bimbambole sofa. Italy. Photo courtesy of the Conran Shop, London.
180 Interior with conversation pit. Photo Elizabeth Whiting & Associates.
181 Pastille chair. Fibreglass and polyester resin. Finnish. 20 × 36 × 36 (50·8 × 91·4 × 91·4). Victoria and Albert Museum, London.
182 Cube-kit furniture designed by Donald Maxwell. Photo Cube Store Ltd, London.
183 Acrylic loudspeaker. Designed by Harwell Instruments and made by Quadrant 4. Early 1970s. Photo Mann Brothers, London.
184 Acrylic nesting tables. Photo courtesy of Albrizzi Ltd, London.
185 Foyer of the Park Tower Hotel, London. Photo courtesy of Richard Seifert and Partners, London.
186 Sycamore and walnut dining-chair. English. Photo courtesy of Rupert Williamson.
187 Ebony and nickel-silver chair. Photo courtesy of John Makepeace.
188 Allen Jones, Table Sculpture. Life-size. The Waddington Galleries, London. Photo A.C. Cooper.
189 Laminated cherrywood settee. North American. 32 × 78 × 36 (81·3 × 198 × 91·4). Photo courtesy of Wendell Castle.

Index

Figures in italic are illustration numbers